NAZI GERMANY

NAZI GERMANY

THE FACE OF TYRANNY

Ted Gottfried

Illustrations by Stephen Alcorn

THE HOLOCAUST
Twenty-First Century Books
Brookfield, Connecticut

Title page and chapter opening illustrations
by Stephen Alcorn© www.alcorngallery.com

Photographs courtesy of Brown Brothers: p. 18; Corbis/Bettmann-UPI: p. 25; Hulton
Getty/Liaison Agency: pp. 39, 46, 69, 97; Süddeutscher Verlag-Bilderdienst: p. 58;
Instytut Pamieci Narodowej/Institute of National Memory, courtesy of USHMM
Photo Archive: pp. 78, 89

Library of Congress Cataloging-in-Publication Data
Gottfried, Ted.
Nazi Germany: the face of tyranny / Ted Gottfried.
p. cm. — (The Holocaust)
Includes bibliographical references and index.
Summary: Describes the Nazis' rise to power in Germany and their efforts to con-
quer Europe, as well as their full-scale war against Jews and others.
ISBN 0-7613-1714-7 (lib. bdg.)
1. Holocaust, Jewish (1939–1945)—Juvenile literature. 2. National socialism—
Juvenile literature. 3. Hitler, Adolf, 1889–1945—Juvenile literature. 4.
Antisemitism—Europe—Juvenile literature. [1. National socialism. 2. Holocaust,
Jewish (1939–1945) 3. Hitler, Adolf, 1889–1945. 4. Antisemitism.] I. Title. II.
Holocaust
(Brookfield, Conn.)
D810.J4 G68 2000
940.53'18—dc21   99-057589

Published by Twenty-First Century Books
A Division of The Millbrook Press, Inc.
2 Old New Milford Road
Brookfield, Connecticut 06804
www.millbrookpress.com

In memory of the Jewish men, women, and children

of Dnepropetrovsk, Ukraine,

who were murdered in the Holocaust.

ACKNOWLEDGMENTS

I am grateful to personnel of the Judaica Room of the New York Central Research Library, the Mid-Manhattan library, the Jewish Museum, and the Holocaust Museum, as well as those at the central branch of the Queensboro Public Library. Thanks are also due to my fellow writers Janet Bode and Kathryn Paulsen, and—with much love—the contribution of my wife, Harriet Gottfried, who—as always—read and critiqued each chapter of this book as it was written.

All contributed, but any shortcomings in the work are mine alone.

—Ted Gottfried

CONTENTS

Introduction
THE HOLOCAUST: AN OVERVIEW

During wars, soldiers kill each other. Cities are bombed and civilians—children, women, sick people, old people—die. War wrecks the lives of those in its way, and helpless people sometimes starve or freeze to death. All of these things happened in World War II. But something even more horrible happened as well.

Six million civilians—men, women, children—were cold-bloodedly, often methodically, murdered according to a program that was planned, revised, and carried out by the Nazis, who ruled Germany at that time. The six million were killed because they were Jews. Those responsible called it "The Final Solution." The world calls it the *Holocaust*.

"Never before had a state . . . decided that a specific human group, including its aged, its women, its children, and its infants, would be killed as quickly as possible and then carried through this regulation using every possible means of state power."[1] That is how German historian Eberhard Jackel defines the Holocaust.

Two thirds of the Jews of Europe were slaughtered. Ninety percent of the Jews of Poland and Lithuania died. The Holocaust wiped out one of every three Jews in the world.

Many years have passed since the Holocaust. Memories of its horrors have faded. Recent polls show that as many as 22 percent of Americans either don't believe the Holocaust really happened, or think that the accounts of it are exaggerated.

Yet few events in history are as well documented as the Holocaust. There are so-called Death Books[2]—records of mass murders of Jews kept by those in charge of carrying them out. There are signed extermination orders, boastful reports of increases in killings, transportation records of the millions of people delivered to their death, bills for the gas used to kill them, records of the furnaces used to get rid of the bodies, even films taken by the Nazis of the murders. And there are the mass graves created by American-made grave-digging machines faced with the problem of disposing of the bones of thousands of corpses.

There are hundreds of carefully kept Nazi records, as well as forty-two volumes of trial evidence filled with the testimony of eyewitnesses—many of them German—documenting the full extent of the Holocaust. The evidence is overwhelming.

The Nazi Pledge

As early as the 1920s, the fringe group on the far, ultra-conservative "right," which would become the Nazi party, was attracting recruits with its promise to make Germany *Judenrein*—rid of Jews—by whatever means necessary. In the 1930s many laws were passed against the Jews. But it was only after World War II started that the full force of making all of Europe Judenrein was put into effect. The Holocaust followed.

As the German army moved east through Poland and deep into Russia, Nazi killing squads followed in their wake. Jews were rounded up and shot, or put in ghettoes and later gassed. In the conquered countries of Western Europe they were herded into boxcars and shipped to death camps.

The Guilty

In many of the conquered countries there were those who collaborated with the Germans in disposing of the Jews. French and Dutch police cooperated in the roundups. Polish towns surrendered their Jewish citizens and seized their property. Ukrainians were organized into firing squads to exterminate Jews and also served as concentration camp guards. The Nazis were responsible, but many others shared the guilt.

Blame may also be laid at the feet of governments of other nations that were neither allied with nor conquered by Germany. The United States, for example, strictly limited the number of Jewish refugees it would admit and the U.S. Coast Guard turned away a ship with almost a thousand Jewish passengers fleeing Germany. In June 1943 both the United States and Britain refused to pay ransom to save some 70,000 Romanian Jews from the death camps. Most other countries turned their backs on the Jews and the Holocaust as well.

The Key Question

There are many questions. Did the "don't get-involved" attitude of the civilized world make it in part responsible for the mass murder of the Jews? What about the German people? Did they know or not know about the Holocaust? Did they go along out of fear of the Nazis or out of hatred of the Jews? Were the Germans dominated by the Nazis or did they support them?

Whatever the answers, the Holocaust was the creation of the Nazis. That raises the key question: How could the Germans—how could the world—have allowed such an evil movement to come to power?

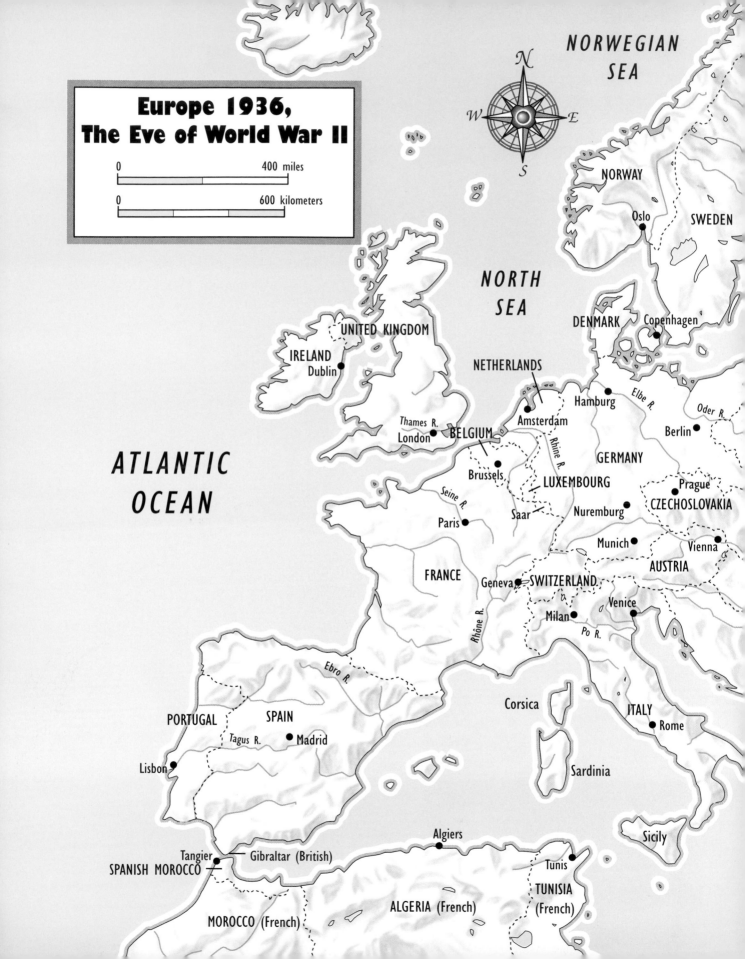

Europe 1936, The Eve of World War II

0 — 400 miles

0 — 600 kilometers

NORWEGIAN SEA

N
W — E
S

NORWAY

Oslo

SWEDEN

NORTH SEA

DENMARK

Copenhagen

UNITED KINGDOM

IRELAND
Dublin

NETHERLANDS

Hamburg

Elbe R.

Oder R.

Amsterdam

Berlin

Thames R.
London

BELGIUM

Brussels

Rhine R.

GERMANY

LUXEMBOURG

Prague

CZECHOSLOVAKIA

Seine R.

Saar

Nuremburg

ATLANTIC OCEAN

Paris

Munich

Vienna

FRANCE

Geneva

SWITZERLAND

AUSTRIA

Venice

Milan

Po R.

Ebro R.

Corsica

ITALY

PORTUGAL

SPAIN

Rome

Tagus R.

Madrid

Lisbon

Sardinia

Sicily

Algiers

Tangier — Gibraltar (British)

SPANISH MOROCCO

Tunis

TUNISIA
(French)

ALGERIA (French)

MOROCCO (French)

"hen I fight against Jews, I am doing the work of the Lord,"[1] declared Adolf Hitler in the 1920s.

The onetime tramp and prison inmate who would become dictator of Germany might have seemed too comic a figure to be taken seriously at the time. He always stood stiffly at attention, as if to deliberately exaggerate his average height and build. When he walked, he never strolled, but seemed always to be marching like a toy soldier on parade.

Hitler's voice could be high and shrill, his gestures like those of a child having a tantrum. His straight, dark hair would fall across his forehead when his anger got the better of him. At such times his image might seem to dissolve into the small, dark smudge of mustache under his nose, which made him look like the famous comic tramp of the movies, Charlie Chaplin.

But the resemblance to Chaplin was misleading. Those who came to Nazi rallies did not laugh when Adolf Hitler spoke. On the contrary, they listened, and they were moved.

Hitler in Action

"Adolf Hitler enters a hall. He sniffs the air, feels his way, senses the atmosphere. Suddenly he bursts forth. His words go like an arrow to their target, he touches each private wound on the raw, liberating the unconscious . . . and telling it what it most wants to hear."[2]

This was the effect that Adolf Hitler had on his audiences in the first days of the Nazi movement according to Otto Strasser, an early follower. Strasser also spoke of Hitler's ability "to act as a loudspeaker proclaiming the most secret desires, the least admissible instincts, the sufferings and personal revolts of a whole nation."[3]

Hitler had heard the song some Germans sang after their country's defeat in World War I: *We Germans did not lose the war. It was the Jews who betrayed us.*[4] Hitler turned the song into a Nazi national anthem.

The Message

The recent defeat of Germany in World War I was a humiliation too great to be borne by a proud people, Hitler told his audiences. The victors had stolen a third of the German nation, he declared, lands rich in minerals, industrial areas, and farms. They had taken from Germany the *Lebensraum* (room to exist) so necessary to the growing German population. Because of this there were no jobs, food shortages, and German money had lost its value.

The Nazi party, Hitler promised, would right these wrongs. The Nazis would give Germany back its pride. They would restore "to the German nation the territory which is due it on this earth."[5]

He blamed greedy businessmen for the depression in the country. He blamed the Communists for the labor battles and food riots. He blamed the German government for not cracking down on the profiteers and the Communists. But above all, he blamed the Jews of Germany—and of the world.

The Jews were only the first of the *Untermenschen*—subhumans—Hitler targeted from the very beginning. Slavs, southern Europeans, and all non-white races were also inferior. The Aryan race—by which he meant the German people—were superior to all others.

All civilization, according to Hitler, was "the creative product of the Aryan."[6] Furthermore, Europe had become civilized only because Aryans had

Vote for the Nazi candidate, this German propaganda poster urged, and do away with the rich Jewish industrialists who control both the workers and the economy.

conquered inferior peoples and ruled over them. In Hitler's view, Aryans must always be the masters and all others the slaves.

Hitler defined his Aryans as a pure race. They had never mixed their blood with any other. (This was not true, but it was widely believed in Germany at that time.) All other races were not pure. All other peoples were mongrels, declared Hitler. Only the Aryans—the German people—were pure of blood, noble of spirit, and qualified to be masters. And what was true of Germany was, of course, true of Hitler himself.

Ein Volk! Ein Reich! Ein Führer![7] ("One people! One nation! One leader!") the Nazis roared. Hitler was embraced by the Nazis, and eventually by millions of other Germans, as the personal living symbol of the nation itself. "The German people loved him,"[8] reports historian Jackel.

There was no doubt about it. Hitler's charisma was dazzling. It takes more than charisma, however, to lay claim to the soul of a nation.

The Great Deceiver

"In all great deceivers a remarkable process is at work," wrote Friedrich Nietzsche, the German philosopher most admired by Hitler. "They are overcome *by their belief in themselves*; it is this belief which then speaks, so persuasively, so miracle-like, to the audience."[9] However, what is spoken is not always the truth. Hitler did not deceive himself about that. He was fanatic and ruthless and he often lied.

His most powerful weapon was propaganda—the words he and other top Nazi speakers and writers used to sway the German people. Propaganda "must present only that aspect of the truth which is favorable to one's own side,"[10] he wrote. "The people," Hitler declared, "must be misled."[11]

2

THE SEEDS OF NAZISM

**W**ere the German people misled?

"Hitler spent twelve years promising the German people that if he came to power he would eliminate the Jews; in 1933 he got in, and he spent the next twelve years living up to his promise. No Germans ever stopped him; few even tried. And, no matter how you look at it, the Germans are responsible for that."[1]

That is one point of view, but there are others.

A woman who grew up as a child in Nazi Germany remembers "how Hitler cleverly seduced the German people by giving them work and bread and a renewed belief in themselves."[2] A historian cautions us "not to repeat the Nazis mistakes [by] labeling groups as demonic,"[3] meaning that if we blame *all* Germans for the Holocaust, then we are saying that *all* Germans are evil, which is just what the Nazis said about the Jews.

The Birth of a Nation

How did Germany get to the point where individual Germans had to say yes or no to the Nazis, or turn their backs on the slaughter? The past may hold the answer. It may be found in the history of two peoples—the Germans and the Jews.

Germany was not really a nation until 1871. Before then it was a collection of states and territories, which sometimes fought with one another and sometimes were allied with one another. It was the Prussian chancellor Otto von Bismarck who brought together these German states in a war against France. After the Franco-German War Bismarck founded a united German Empire to be ruled by Kaiser Wilhelm I of the royal house of Hohenzollern.

There had been Jews in Germany long before that. They had fled there from Spain and France and Holland and Belgium just as they had fled to those countries from Muslim lands, and just as they had fled from Germany and Austria to Poland and Russia in times of trouble.

Initially, the Jews fled the religious wars, which have occurred throughout history. One reason these wars were fought was to convert a person to a particular religion, or to kill such a person as an agent of the devil because he or she denied the god of that religion. Muslims killed Christians, and Christians killed Muslims. Catholics killed Protestants, and Protestants killed Catholics. And they all killed the Jews.

There were much fewer of them. They didn't want to convert to some other religion. Some were killed because of this, and some because they got in the way of other religions battling each other. Because Jewish groups were too small to fight, they had three choices: die, convert, or leave. Many did die, and some did convert. But the majority moved on, and then moved on again.

In this way, the Jews came to Germany. Some kept on going to other lands to the east. Some stayed in Germany.

The Ghettoes

When Jews arrived, the land in Germany was already owned. Peasants were already doing the work on the farms and there was little need for more workers. Shut out from being landowners or workers, the Jews became merchants and storekeepers.

As non-Germans, their activities were restricted. Jews were forbidden to own property. They had to rent homes in specific areas, which came to be known as ghettoes. The ghettoes had substandard housing, poor sanitary facilities, and were sometimes surrounded by high walls. These walls, and the fact that the buildings tended to be both narrow and high, kept out the sunlight. Overcrowded housing resulted in high disease rates in the ghettoes. Jews could not move about surrounding areas freely and had to return to these ghettoes before dark. There were other laws, many petty, which applied only to them.

Jews were different from ordinary Germans. They had different customs. They worshiped differently. They dressed differently, wearing skullcaps, prayer shawls, or other clothing associated with their religion. Because they were herded together in ghettoes, these differences were magnified.

The Very German Jews

In the early part of the nineteenth century, some individual German states relaxed the laws restricting Jews. Toward the end of the century, after Germany became a nation, there was a nationwide lifting—in stages—of such restrictions. By 1900, Jews, while still subject to some minor restrictions, were better off under German law than in most European countries of that period. They could own property and they could engage in business. Although many Jews during this period were forced to remain living in the ghettoes because they didn't have enough money to leave, many others—particularly merchants—were now able to improve themselves and to become part of the German middle class. Many poor Germans, peasants and workers, resented this.

They fueled this resentment by assuring each other that these Jews had succeeded only by lying, cheating, and stealing. They added that the Jews in the ghettoes were all wealthy and stayed there because it was in their Jewish nature to live in filth while hoarding their gold. Legally, the Jews may now have been full German citizens, but there was still much prejudice against them.

On the whole, however, the Jews of Germany became good Germans. They embraced the culture—the music, the literature, the traditions—of the nation. They listened to the symphonies of Beethoven. They read the poems of Goethe. They cheered when the Prussian cavalry marched on parade.

Jewish men gather on a street in the heart of the Berlin ghetto in 1923.

They were patriotic. During World War I, Jews served in the German army in large numbers. Some were officers. Many Jews won medals, including the top honor of all, the Iron Cross.

True, there were sometimes pamphlets written attacking the Jews. Every now and then there was violence against them by hoodlums. But these were exceptions, not the rule of daily life. On the whole, during the first years of the twentieth century, the Jews were content in Germany. They were as proud to be Germans as they were to be Jews.

The Bitter Defeat

Bravery was not enough. World War I ended in November 1918, and Germany's defeat was bitter. The Germans had imposed harsh terms on the French when they won the Franco-German War in 1871, and now was a time of revenge.

During World War I, the British and American navies had stopped ships from reaching German seaports. These ships had carried not only war supplies, but food as well. Between the time the war ended and the time the Treaty of Versailles (peace agreement) was signed at the end of June 1919, "the naval blockade not only continued but tightened,"[4] writes professor of history Donald S. Detwiler.

Detwiler adds that at the end of the war Germany handed over to the victors "150,000 freight cars and 5,000 locomotives in addition to 5,000 trucks."[5] Few vehicles were left to carry food to the German people. Food could not be transported by land or sea. When millions of German soldiers were released from the army, they swelled the ranks of those for whom there was not enough food. During the winter of 1918–1919, there was "widespread starvation"[6] in Germany.

Many stores that ordinarily would have sold food and other necessities were owned by Jews—the descendants of those forced to become merchants by the laws that had once forbidden them to own property or to take jobs that non-Jews might fill. These Jewish shopkeepers were caught between empty shelves and selling scarce goods from suppliers who charged high prices, which had to be passed along to their customers. Either way, there were those who blamed the Jews for the shortage of food and accused them of getting rich from it.

Now there was also talk that the Jews were to blame for Germany having lost the war. Jewish arms manufacturers, it was whispered, had overcharged the government for weapons and ammunition and had supplied inferior equipment, which had cost many brave German boys their lives. Jewish bankers, it was muttered, had charged such unreasonably high interest on government loans that Germany had been squeezed dry of the money it needed to wage the war.

In fact, almost all arms manufacturers supplying the German army were large German and Austro-Hungarian firms. Most of the banks were German owned. The loans from those few owned by Jews were at the same rate as from those owned by Germans.

Despite the mutterings, the anti-Jewish songs, and the occasional bullying of individual Jews in the streets by gangs of rowdies, most Germans were not focused on blaming the Jews for the nation's troubles after the war. They were far more likely to blame those who won the war. Most of all, and for years to come, they blamed the peace agreement which they believed had been shoved down their throats by the victors. They blamed the Treaty of Versailles.

Signed in the Hall of Mirrors at the Palace of Versailles where Queen Marie Antoinette of France had once held court, the treaty officially ending World War I contained "the seeds of trouble [for Germany] for the next twenty years."[7] It surrendered German territory to Belgium, France, Poland, Czechoslovakia, Lithuania, and Denmark. Germany lost one seventh of its national territory, including the coal-rich Saar and many manufacturing regions. In addition, all of Germany's overseas colonies were taken over by the victors.

Germany and its allies were to pay all the costs of the war. The victorious nations and their citizens were to be paid back in full for losses and damages suffered because of "the war imposed upon them by the aggression of Germany and her allies."[8] An "Allied Reparation Committee"[9] was set up to decide just how much Germany would have to pay. For starters, the committee decided that all property owned by German citizens abroad and in the former German colonies would be seized by the victors, and the German government would have full responsibility for paying the owners for it.

The treaty forbid Germany to draft citizens into its military forces. The sizes of the army and navy were strictly limited—100,000 men for the army—as were the amounts and types of weapons the military was allowed to have. Germany was forbidden to have any air force at all. The general staff, which had been in charge of waging the war, was removed from its various posts and forbidden to return to them. Manufacture of weapons was also limited.

There was to be international control of German rivers. The victors were to be allowed to fly over Germany at will. Certain areas west of the Rhine River were to be occupied by the victors' troops for between five and fifteen years.

Kaiser Wilhelm II, who at the beginning of the war had ordered his troops to invade neutral Belgium in order to attack France, was directed under the terms of the treaty to stand trial before a special court for "a supreme offense against international morality and the sanctity of treaties."[10] By then the German people had little love left for the kaiser. The effect of the Treaty of Versailles on the German economy was immediately devastating. The harsh terms of the treaty seemed a deliberate insult to the German people. The cowardly flight of the kaiser had been the beginning of their humiliation.

Blamed for the nation's costly defeats in battle, Kaiser Wilhelm II had fled Germany on November 9, 1918, two days before the end of the war. He had gone to Holland, which later refused to surrender him to stand trial. The kaiser left behind a nation on the brink of revolution.

The most powerful group behind the call for revolution modeled itself on the Bolsheviks of 1917, who had taken over Russia after the czar was overthrown and replaced the revolutionary democratic government with a

Communist regime. In Germany they called themselves Spartacists, after Spartacus, the leader of the slave rebellion in ancient Rome. They wanted to set up a workers' state, using whatever force was necessary.

They were stopped by a coalition of antirevolution parties headed by the so-called Majority Social Democrats. The coalition formed a Council of People's Representatives and elected the socialist Friedrich Ebert as chairman. The council set a date for elections for a democratic assembly to rule Germany and obtained a pledge from General Paul von Hindenburg to use the army to put down any attempts at revolution.

Nevertheless, throughout January 1919, pitched battles were fought with the Spartacists and other groups opposed to the elections. There were bitter clashes with partisan groups along the Polish border. In many German cities—particularly Berlin and Munich—the streets ran with blood.

The Weimar Republic

The elections went ahead as planned, and the democratic assembly, which would be known as the *Reichstag*, was formed on January 19, 1919. It met in the city of Weimar on February 6, and Friedrich Ebert was named president of Germany. The Reichstag's first task was to write a constitution for the new republic. It was finished and signed into law in August of that year.

However, to establish a republic and to make it work are two different things. To rule over a population that would suffer for many years to come from the effects of the Treaty of Versailles was "the fatal weakness of the Weimar Republic: From its very origin it had lacked broad popular backing or even the strong support of the elite."[11]

Opposition to the Weimar government came from both the left and the right. In 1920 a right-wing attempt to overthrow the republic came close to success when the army refused to protect it. The government was forced to flee from Berlin to Stuttgart. A takeover of the country "was only defeated by a solid working class resistance and the organization by the trade unions of a general strike."[12]

The Weimar Republic stood, but the turmoil continued. The German economy was in shreds; German money was worthless; the people were suffering. They couldn't buy food and clothing with money, so they bartered for the necessities of daily living. The violent riots persisted throughout the first years of the 1920s.

The Beer Hall Putsch

In October 1923, Communists led an uprising in Hamburg, which was put down by the German army. There was organized Communist opposition against the republic in the German states of Saxony and Thuringia. A leftist government in Bavaria openly defied the government of the Weimar Republic.

Meanwhile, in Munich, the threat came not from the left, but from the misleadingly named National Socialist German Workers party (Nazis)—an anti-Communist, anti-Jewish, strongly nationalist group, which demanded the overthrow of the Weimar Republic. On the evening of November 8, a gathering of some three thousand Munich businessmen was being addressed by a government official at a local beer hall when a band of armed National Socialists took over the meeting. Their leader jumped up on a table and fired his revolver at the ceiling. "The national revolution has begun!" he shouted.[13]

The next day it was over. The armed band had attempted to march on the War Ministry where some of their comrades were surrounded by soldiers. Their ultimate aim had been to convince the Munich government and all able-bodied citizens to join them in a march on "that sinful Babel,"[14] Berlin, to overthrow the government of the Weimar Republic. At the head of the march, alongside the rebel leader, was General Erich Ludendorff, a popular hero of World War I.

Their way was blocked by a battalion of police. A shot rang out. A volley of crossfire followed. When the smoke cleared, sixteen Nazis and three policemen were dead. General Ludendorff was arrested.

The leader of the rebels, however, had fled. When the shooting started, according to several witnesses, he "was the first to get up and turn back."[15] It was only later that he was caught, tried, and sent to jail. By then he had become famous throughout Germany.

His name was Adolf Hitler.

3

**BORN TO
BE A
DICTATOR**

"The man who is born to be a dictator"[1] was how Hitler described himself during the trial following the failed 1923 rebellion they called the Beer Hall Putsch. His birth took place on April 20, 1889. The future German dictator was not born in Germany, but in Branau, Austria. He was the third child of his father's third marriage.

Adolf's mother, Klara Poelzl, was twenty-two years younger than his father when they married. His parents' first two children—a boy and a girl—died before Adolf was born. Adolf's younger brother, Edmund, died at the age of six. Only Adolf and a younger sister, Clara, survived to adulthood. Adolf also had an older half brother and half sister from his father's previous marriages.

Because of his father's job as a customs officer for the Austro-Hungarian Empire, Adolf's family often moved from place to place. During the years he was growing up, there were seven such moves. The boy was sent to five different schools.

His father was very strict with Adolf. He bullied the boy. But Adolf's mother doted on him and spoiled him. She also sang to him and encouraged him to sing along with her. Adolf had a good voice. He took singing lessons. He sang in the choir of a Benedictine monastery where he also attended classes for two years. Describing this period of his life, Hitler told how he "dreamed of one day taking holy orders."[2]

When he was eleven years old, his ambition changed. He entered a private high school in Linz and realized that he had a talent for drawing. Soon he was painting as well, and he decided that he would make a career for himself as an artist. "My father was struck speechless," Hitler remembered. " 'Painter? Artist?' He doubted my sanity. . . . 'Artist! No! Never as long as I live!' "[3] He wanted Adolf to follow in his footsteps and become a civil servant.

Adolf, however, was determined. Where once he had earned average marks in school, he now began to fail every subject except drawing and gymnastics. "I thought that once my father saw how little progress I was making at high school he would let me devote myself to my dream, whether he liked it or not,"[4] he explained.

Actually, young Adolf preferred playing war games and reading cowboy novels to doing schoolwork. He was thrown out of one school because of failing grades, but did little better in the next two schools he attended. Nor did his grades improve after his father's death shortly before Adolf's fourteenth birthday. Adolf's teachers continued to describe him as "idle, willful and disrespectful."[5]

Lessons Learned in Vienna

When he was sixteen years old, Adolf persuaded his mother to let him quit school and go to Vienna to take the test for admission to the Vienna Academy of Arts. His mother supported him in Vienna for two years while he put off taking the test. Adolf bought himself an ivory-topped ebony walking stick and strutted around Vienna like a young aristocrat.

Through a friend he discovered the operas of Richard Wagner and he went to see them as often as possible. Hitler identified with Wagner's German superheroes. He also read about Wagner, admired him, and may have been drawn to the composer's well-known anti-Semitism (hatred of Jews).

There had been no hatred of Jews in the Hitler household. His mother and father expressed no feelings against Jews and passed none on to Adolf. "At home

I do not remember having heard the word [Jew] during my father's lifetime," Hitler recalled. He did remember one Jewish boy in high school, "but we didn't give the matter any thought."

Vienna was another story. When Hitler was there the population of the city was around two million, of which roughly 175,000 were Jews. They were approximately 8.6 percent of the population, and they were very prominent in the fields of education, medicine, journalism, and the performing arts. Most of them, however, were poor and lived in the city's two ghettoes.

There were two political parties with anti-Semitic platforms. One was the Christian Social party to which the *burgomaster*—head of the Vienna government—belonged. The other was the Pan-German Nationalist party which also preached German superiority over all other nationalities in the Austro-Hungarian Empire. Hitler attended meetings of both parties and embraced their anti-Jewish and pro-German messages.

"Vienna appeared to me in a new light," he wrote. "Was there any shady undertaking, any form of foulness . . . in which at least one Jew did not participate?"[6]

The Struggling Young Artist

In 1907, Hitler finally applied for admission to the Academy of Arts, but was rejected. He continued living on money his mother sent him. He loafed. He attended right-wing political lectures. He went to the opera and soaked up Wagnerian fantasies.

This comfortable life was shattered by the death of his mother later that year. She left him a little money, but it was soon used up. He tried for admission to the academy again, but was again turned down. This time he was told quite bluntly that he lacked the necessary talent to be an artist.

By the autumn of 1909, Hitler was flat broke. He couldn't pay the back rent on his room. Soon he was sleeping on park benches and in doorways and standing in line for free soup from church kitchens. Finally he was given a bed in a homeless shelter.

At first he had begged for handouts, but then he started to copy watercolors from photographs of Viennese landmarks and peddled them to tourists. He joined a group of homeless men who called themselves "intellectuals,"[7] but rarely took part in their discussions. However, when the talk turned political, Hitler would leap to his feet and shout his anti-Semitic, pro-German views.

In 1913, at age twenty-four, Hitler became eligible to be drafted into the Austro-Hungarian army. Hitler had been born in Austria and lived in Austria, but he always considered himself a German. He believed, as did many ethnic Germans who lived in Austria, that German ancestry was superior. Hitler avoided the Austrian draft by fleeing to Munich, Germany.

When World War I broke out in 1914, Hitler enlisted in the German army. He was promoted to corporal, but any further promotions "were denied him because he was not considered a potential leader."[8] Even so, he was wounded and awarded the Iron Cross First Class for bravery.

Hitler remained in the army for a short while after the war ended. At a political forum given for the troops, a soldier asked why Germany had lost the war. The company commander ordered Hitler to write a reply.

He blamed the Jews. He wrote that they had infected Germany with a racial tuberculosis that had cost the Fatherland the war. Hitler recommended the establishment of "a government of national power" whose "ultimate goal . . . must absolutely be the removal of the Jews altogether."[9]

From Mole to Mouthpiece

Assigned as an "army political agent,"[10] Hitler joined a small fringe group called the Germany Workers' party,[11] which was active in Munich. Less than a year later he left the army to devote all his time to building up the party's membership. He was put in charge of propaganda. One of his first acts was to rename the party "*Nationalsozialistische Deutsche Arbeiterpartei,*"[12] which was abbreviated to *Nazi*.

From the first, Hitler showed a genius for giving voice to the party's principles. He had the knack of relating the party's twenty-five-point program, which he had helped to write in February 1920, to the postwar suffering and feelings of the average German. In particular he stressed Point Four, which declared that "no Jew may be a member of the [German] nation."[13]

Mein Kampf

Despite Hitler's efforts, the Nazi party grew slowly in the early 1920s. It could claim only two to three thousand members in 1923 when the Beer Hall Putsch landed Hitler in prison. He served nine months, during which time he wrote his autobiography, *Mein Kampf* (*My Struggle*), a highly dramatized view of his life up to that point. The details were mixed with anti-Semitic propaganda deliberately worded to provoke violence against German Jews. He told his readers that millions of "real Germans" might not have died in World War I if "twelve or fifteen thousand of these Hebrew corrupters of the people had been held under poison gas."[14]

Mein Kampf came out in 1925. It was not a best-seller immediately—9,473 copies sold that first year—but sales held steady through the 1920s, and royalties from them supported Hitler while he continued working to build up the Nazi party. The year he became chancellor, sales of *Mein Kampf* in Germany zoomed to over a million copies.

The points stressed in the book were also stressed by Hitler in the late 1920s as he recruited for the Nazi party. By 1928 the party had 108,717 members, but Hitler personally could claim countless followers who were not party members. Among them were wealthy German businessmen and industrialists "who controlled political funds and were anxious to use them to establish a strong right-wing, anti-working-class government,"[15] which would crack down on the Communist movement in Germany.

Adolf Hitler
in 1925

The Nazi Vote

In 1929, Germany, like much of the world, was thrown into a depression. The people were hurting and the government of the Weimar Republic wasn't helping. Increasingly the choice seemed to be between the Nazis on the right and the Communists on the left. Hitler made an alliance with the German Nationalist People's party—a wealthy right-wing party, which let him spread his Nazi message in the pages of the many newspapers it controlled.

Due to Hitler's rising popularity, the Nazis received over six million votes in the 1930 election, making them the second largest party in Germany. "His appeal," says Hitler's biographer Alan Bullock, "cut across class, regional and religious boundaries, affecting both young and old, men and women."[16] During the next two years Hitler built on that appeal.

His efforts translated into still more votes. The winner of the 1932 election was the aging war hero Field Marshal General Paul von Hindenburg. Hitler came in second, receiving 36.8 percent of the votes. Hitler's popularity was so strong that if Hindenburg was going to be able to govern, he would have to do so in partnership with him. In January 1933, Hindenburg grudgingly appointed Hitler chancellor of Germany.

In this position, with the Nazi movement growing, Hitler persuaded the Reichstag to give him control over more and more of the government. When President Hindenburg died in August 1934, the Nazis had enough votes in the Reichstag to merge the offices of president and chancellor. Adolf Hitler—legally and constitutionally—became the dictator of the German nation.

The former Vienna tramp with the Chaplin mustache was now officially the leader—*Der Führer*—of Germany.

4 THE NAZI MOVEMENT: THEORIES AND THUGS

dolf Hitler was neither one of the first leaders of the Nazi party nor its founder. It was started just before the end of World War I by Anton Drexler, a locksmith who worked in the railroad shops of Munich. It began as the "Committee of Independent Workmen"[1] opposed to communism and trade unions. From the first it was anti-Semitic. Its main goal was a fair settlement of the war for Germany, but this was not to be.

Drexler was a poorly educated man who wore thick glasses and was described as "sickly."[2] He was "a poor writer and a worse speaker."[3] He had a hard time attracting people to his cause and the committee's membership was never more than forty, many of whom were inactive.

In January 1919, Drexler's group merged with the Political Workers Circle. The new group called itself the German Workers' Party. The combined membership still totaled less than a hundred. The new party's chairman was Karl Harrer, a newspaper reporter. Today Harrer is remembered for his early description of Hitler as a "poor speaker"[4]—a judgment history denies.

One of the early members of the party was Ernst Röhm, a former captain in the German army. Röhm had been wounded three times in the war. The upper part of his nose had been shot away. He was a brutal street fighter who had organized a "private strong-arm force,"[5] which fought bloody battles with Social Democrats, Communists, and trade unionists in the streets of Munich.

Röhm believed, as would Hitler, that a strong Germany could only be rebuilt by a political party that drew its support from the lower classes. He recruited his followers from the unemployed, from discharged German soldiers, and from the ranks of homosexual men. Röhm was himself a homosexual, a fact that would later be used as an excuse for the bloodbath that ended his life.

After Hitler joined the party, Röhm used his contacts among the officer class in Bavaria to win support for the Nazi cause. This meant that the army either would not interfere in the battles between the Nazis and other groups or would find ways to back them up. In October 1921, Röhm officially brought his followers into the party as the *Sturmabteilung* (storm troopers) where they became known as the SA, or "Brownshirts,"[6] because of the uniforms they wore.

Brains Not Needed

If Röhm provided the brawn for the party, Dietrich Eckart was its brains. Eckart, twenty-one years older than Hitler, was both a father figure and a teacher to him. Often, Eckart was called "the spiritual founder"[7] of Nazism. In *Mein Kampf*, Hitler credited Eckart with shaping his ideas.

What were these ideas? At war's end, in the beer halls of Munich, Eckart preached Aryan superiority, called for the elimination of the Jews from German society, and ranted against the *Schwein* (pigs) forming the new Weimar government in Berlin. Hitler, of course, agreed with all of this. But it was Eckart who developed the logic and structure for the Nazi program, which Hitler turned into reality.

A journalist, poet, and dramatist who never had any of his plays produced, Eckart was brilliant but unstable. He had been a drunkard, taken morphine, and been confined to a mental institution. He had declared that the "rabble"[8] required a leader who "doesn't need much brains,"[9] adding that "he must be a bachelor, then we'll get the women."[10] In Eckart's eyes, Hitler may have been this leader.

Pre-Nazi Anti-Semitism

While Eckart and Hitler were fine-tuning the Nazi philosophy, anti-Semitism was already on the rise in postwar Germany. This was not at first a result of Nazi activity, but it did fit in neatly with Nazi ideas. In the summer of 1920, Hitler came up with the symbol for those ideas—the swastika—and it quickly became the symbol of Jewish persecution as well.

Hitler fashioned it as a flag for the new Nazi party and outlined the design in black, white, and bloodred. It soon appeared on flags during anti-Jewish demonstrations, both those provoked by the Nazis and others. At this time, between the end of the World War I and 1923, "a large number of government reports from around Germany [describe] a virulent hatred of Jews."[11] In March 1920 the head of a German district government wrote that "one hears everywhere that 'our government is delivering us over to the Jews.' "[12] In 1921 a Munich police summary warned that "the mood for Jewish *pogroms* [massacres] is spreading systematically in all parts of the country."[13]

There was a flare-up of anti-Semitism in the schools and universities. Education was as much a part of the Jewish culture as symphony music was of the German heritage. There were many Jewish professors and teachers and many Jewish students in German institutions. Now they were under attack.

As early as 1920, long before the Nazis had any power, a two-thirds majority of students attending the Technical University of Hanover voted that "students of Jewish descent"[14] be excluded from the Union of German Students. That same year the Prussian minister of science, art, and popular education warned of "a massive swelling of anti-Semitic tendencies at our universities."[15] In many schools students voted that "Aryan paragraphs,"[16] which would exclude Jews, be added to the bylaws of student organizations. As the Nazis gained followers, student leaders began wearing swastikas and distributing anti-Semitic propaganda. Some professors gave anti-Semitic lectures.

The middle-class students and professors of the high schools and universities were not, however, the Nazis' primary targets. It was the workers they wanted to recruit. In the party strategy shaped by Eckart and Hitler, the struggle was between Nazism and communism, nationalism and internationalism, the pure Aryan Germans and the inferior races of the world.

A low level of education, bitterness over a lost war and an unjust treaty, a mistrust of the trade unions, which (in their eyes) had failed to protect their jobs, a belief in the inferiority of non-Germans, and the rage of anti-Semitism—these were the raw materials of the Nazi recruits. Hitler would speak to their emotions. The party would work on their feelings and prejudices and forge them into a mighty destructive force.

The *Voelkischer Beobachter*, an anti-Semitic newspaper the Nazis bought in 1920 and published as a daily, was an important tool in this effort. Its circulation grew and attracted new members to the party when Alfred Rosenberg became its editor. Eckart had introduced Rosenberg to Hitler, who was impressed by Rosenberg's "learning."[17]

Rosenberg, author of *The Myth of the Twentieth Century*, which dealt with race and culture, was a Russian intellectual who had fled the Communists and claimed to be of pure German stock. Before long he was being hailed as the "philosopher"[18] of the Nazi party because of his pompous theories on racial purity and the danger Jews posed to Germany. Another prominent Nazi, Joseph Goebbels, however, dismissed Rosenberg's writing as "an ideological belch."[19]

Goebbels probably preferred *Der Sturmer (The Storm Trooper)*, "the most notorious of all anti-Semitic publications."[20] *Der Sturmer* was put out by Julius Streicher, a Nuremberg elementary school teacher with a low IQ who carried a whip everywhere he went. The publication, which some people considered obscene, featured lurid fantasies of Jewish sex crimes and trumped-up stories of ceremonies involving human sacrifices.

Party Rivalry

Streicher and Rosenberg were not just loyal to the Nazi party, they were loyal to Hitler personally. This was also true of Rudolf Hess, a fanatic who believed

Hitler (far left) and visitors, including Rudolf Hess (second from right), during Hitler's imprisonment following the Beer Hall Putsch

Germany needed a leader who "does not shrink before bloodshed, [a leader] prepared to trample on his closest friends."[21] Hess "showed a doglike devotion to Hitler."[22] When Hitler was serving his jail term for the Beer Hall Putsch, Hess, who had fled to Austria, voluntarily returned to share his imprisonment. He served as Hitler's orderly and secretary in prison. One day Hess would become the number three Nazi, second in line to succeed *Der Führer*.

While Hitler was dictating *Mein Kampf* to Hess in prison, rival forces were at work in the Nazi party. They were led by Gregor Strasser, a former army lieutenant who, like Hitler, had won the Iron Cross. Strasser, who would not take seriously Hitler's claim to be the sole leader of the party, filled the void Hitler had left and organized the Nazis to take part in Bavarian elections. His efforts resulted in two million votes, giving them thirty-two seats in the Reichstag, one of them held by Strasser.

When Hitler emerged from prison, a big rally was held in his honor in Munich. Strasser, pointedly, did not attend it. General Ludendorff and Ernst Röhm had also broken with Hitler. Although furious, Hitler faced reality. Strasser had set up alliances with many right-wing nationalist groups in Hitler's absence. If the party was to stay strong there must not be a split. Hitler made his peace with Strasser and sent him off to northern Germany to recruit new Nazis and organize a new branch of the party.

The chief difference between Strasser and Hitler was that Strasser held Socialist beliefs and saw socialism (combined with nationalism and anti-Semitism) as the best way to fight the still strong Communist threat. Hitler was more practical. The money that the party needed to grow came from rich capitalists eager to fight communism. They were as opposed to socialism as they were to communism and trade unions. It was all very well to lure laborers to the Nazi party with talk of Socialist benefits, but the party could never actively campaign for workers' rights if it was to continue being funded by their bosses.

The Fat Man's Fat Cats

The most effective fund-raiser for the party and the man who put Hitler in contact with the wealthy businessmen and industrialists who financed him was the fattest of the Nazi leaders, Hermann Göring. The overweight Göring had been an ace fighter pilot and commander in the famous Flying Circus Squadron of Baron von Richthofen during World War I. He had joined the Nazi party late in 1922. At the beginning of that year he had met the Swedish baroness Carin von Rosen, who divorced her husband to marry Göring.

Severely wounded in the groin during the Beer Hall Putsch, Göring fled with his wife to Austria. Here his pain was so intense that doctors treated it with morphine and he became addicted to the drug. Throughout 1925 and 1926, he was in and out of mental hospitals in Sweden in an effort to overcome the addiction.

Despite this problem, Göring was a man of great charm. He was much admired as a war hero. Through his aristocratic wife he gained admission to the most elite social circles. In Sweden, he and Carin entertained royalty, government ministers, and top financiers. By the time he returned to Germany in 1927, he had contacts among the most influential businessmen in the country. He remained loyal to Hitler throughout the feud with Strasser, and he convinced many of the wealthy tycoons he came in contact with that Nazism was the most effective answer to their fears of a Communist uprising. The money Göring raised for the Nazi party propelled it from the fringe of politics to the center of power.

The Flip-Flop Flunky

Perhaps the most unlikely Nazi to emerge at that center was Joseph Goebbels. A "dwarfish young man"[23] whom a childhood disease had left with one leg shorter than the other, he had a Ph.D. in philology (the study of language) from Heidelberg University and preferred to be known as "Dr. Goebbels." His disability had kept him out of the army during the war and the rejection made him bitter.

Goebbels's bitterness led him to a 1922 Nazi meeting in Munich, where he heard Hitler speak. "At that moment I was reborn,"[24] Goebbels recorded. He joined the party, but did not rise in its ranks until after the Beer Hall Putsch.

While Hitler was in jail, Gregor Strasser made Goebbels his secretary. Strasser became impressed with Goebbels's ability to write effective propaganda and then with his power as a speaker. He saw that Goebbels had a Hitlerlike ability when it came to swaying audiences.

Goebbels agreed with Strasser's Socialist views. Indeed, he went even further. Goebbels published an open letter to a Communist leader declaring that "Nazism and Communism were really the same thing,"[25] and suggesting that they should join forces instead of fighting each other. As for the jailed Hitler, Goebbels demanded that he "be expelled from the Nazi Party!"[26]

When Hitler got out of prison and decided not to fight Strasser head on, he ignored Goebbels's challenge to his authority. Instead, Hitler set out to lure Goebbels back to the fold. He invited him to speak on the same platform with him in Munich.

"I speak for two and a half hours," Goebbels wrote in his diary. "People roar and shout. At the end Hitler embraces me. I feel happy."[27] He flip-flopped no more. From that day until the day he died, Goebbels remained loyal to Hitler.

At this time, late 1926, the Nazis were gaining support throughout much of Germany, but not in Berlin. Here Röhm's SA thugs were brawling in the street with left-wingers and most Berliners were disgusted with them. The majority of Berliners voted for Socialists and Communists, which made Hitler regard Berlin as hopelessly "red"—under the influence of radicals. He appointed the twenty-nine-year-old Goebbels *Gauleiter* (Nazi commander) of Berlin with the job of bringing the SA under control and Nazifying the city in an orderly fashion. Balancing disciplined force with effective propaganda, Goebbels did this job so well that he became one of the leading lights of the Nazi party.

Hitler's Bodyguards

A year earlier, in 1925, Hitler had become concerned that Röhm might put his Brownshirts at the disposal of Strasser and forcibly remove him from power, or even assassinate him. As protection, Hitler organized the *Schutzstaffel* (guard detachment) to act as his personal bodyguard. Known as the SS, this group would later be expanded and would play a major role in the Holocaust.

Members of the SS wore high boots and black uniforms similar to those worn by Italian dictator Benito Mussolini's Fascist troops. SS members had to swear an oath of loyalty to Hitler personally. In 1929, Hitler named Heinrich Himmler SS commander.

Himmler had been a chicken farmer in a village near Munich. He was an unassuming man with a kindly manner and a quick, friendly smile. There was nothing military in his manner. When he took over the SS, it numbered two hundred men. Himmler expanded it to 10,000 by the end of the year, and to 50,000 by 1933. The Brownshirts no longer posed a serious physical threat to Hitler's safety.

In fact, it was about to be the other way around.

5
THE NAZIS TAKE OVER

"The chess game for power begins," wrote Joseph Goebbels in his diary in January 1932. "There is a man . . . that no one trusts," he recorded. "This is Gregor Strasser."[1]

In the struggle for power, Hitler was busy running for president of Germany against three other candidates. The favorite was General Paul von Hindenburg, who was running for a second term.

The election took place on March 13, 1932, at a time when five million Germans were out of work. Hindenburg got the most votes, but he did not get the majority needed to win the election. Hitler came in second with 30.1 percent of the 37,532,013 votes cast.

There was a runoff vote on April 10 in which Hindenburg got 53 percent of the votes, enough to reelect him as president of Germany. Hitler, however, picked up two million votes and received 36.8 percent of the votes cast. The Nazis were now a strong minority in the Reichstag. They sat all together in their uniforms and upset any proceedings that were not to their liking.

On August 30 the Nazis made a deal with members of smaller parties in the Reichstag and elected Hermann Göring as Reichstag leader. Göring led the successful fight to vote Franz von Papen, the man President Hindenburg had appointed as chancellor, out of office. The stage was now set for Hitler to be named chancellor—a position that in 1930s Germany was more powerful than that of the president.

Hitler Comes to Power

The obstacle was the eighty-four-year-old President von Hindenburg. He loathed Hitler. He would not make Hitler chancellor, he wrote, because the result would be a Nazi "party dictatorship."[2] Instead he named General Kurt von Schleicher as chancellor.

General von Schleicher lasted only fifty-seven days as chancellor. During this time he offered to make Hitler's rival, Nazi leader Gregor Strasser, vice-chancellor. Strasser was willing, and Hitler was furious. This widened the split between the pro-Strasser and pro-Hitler forces in the Nazi party. The chancellor thought the split had solved the Nazi problem, that the Nazis would destroy their party by fighting with each other. He withdrew the offer to Strasser.

But he was wrong. Hitler had made contact with President von Hindenburg's son, Oskar. A witness to the meeting judged that Hitler had succeeded in getting Oskar under his spell. Oskar convinced his father that if Hitler was not made chancellor, it would lead to revolution in Germany. On January 28, 1933, General von Schleicher resigned and on January 30, the aging von Hindenburg gave in and named Hitler chancellor.

At this time the Nazis and the Communists were fighting bloody battles in the streets of many German cities. Hitler announced that he had "advanced with his shock troops and placed himself at the head of the government to lead the German people to liberty."[3] In Berlin large crowds cheered storm troopers in a torchlight parade as they goose-stepped through the Brandenburg Gate, marching with knees pushed high and hips thrust out so that they did indeed look like a flock of waddling geese. Despite their martial strutting, Communists attacked a band of one hundred Nazis and killed one of them as well as a police officer.

The Reichstag Fire

On the night of February 27, 1933, less than a month after Hitler became chancellor, the Reichstag building was set on fire. The flames leaped high from the roof and from all the windows. The building was destroyed, the chamber where the Reichstag met reduced to ashes.

"Now you can see what Germany and Europe have to look for from Communism,"[4] was Hitler's response. A young Dutch Communist named Marinus van der Lubbe was quickly arrested and charged with arson. He was later executed.

But was he guilty? Was the fire an accident? The fire was—and is—"widely believed to have been contrived by the newly formed Nazi government itself to turn public opinion against its opponents and to enable the Nazis to assume emergency powers."[5] The newly named propaganda minister, Joseph Goebbels, was supposedly behind the scheme. It was said to have been executed by a Nazi gang, which got into the Reichstag building by a secret tunnel connecting it with the house of Reichstag president Hermann Göring.

The day after the fire, Hitler issued a decree "for the Protection of the People and the State"[6] that did away with political rights. On March 23 the Reichstag passed the oddly named Enabling Act, which transferred its powers to Hitler's cabinet. Members of the cabinet, of course, had all been put there by Hitler. The effect of the vote—444 to 94—was to make Hitler dictator of Germany.

Under Nazi Law

Hitler named Hermann Göring minister of the interior for the state of Prussia. In this post Göring created the *Geheime Staatspolizei* (secret state police) "to eliminate political opponents."[7] Soon to be taken over and expanded as part of the SS by Heinrich Himmler, it would become known to the world as the *Gestapo*.

Göring also came up with the idea for concentration camps to relieve overcrowding in the jails. Again he turned to Himmler, who built the first camp to house some 15,000 political prisoners arrested in Prussia. It was built at an old gunpowder factory in a town ten miles outside of Munich. The name of the town was Dachau.

On April 1, 1933, government billboards went up all over Germany. "Do not buy from Jews!"[8] was the message. It was backed up by anti-Semitic speeches by Hitler's recently appointed propaganda minister, Goebbels.

The following month huge bonfires were lit in front of universities throughout Germany. They were fueled with so-called "un-German"[9] books. Among them were works by Thomas Mann, Sigmund Freud, Albert Einstein, and Nobel Prize winners Gustav Hertz and James Franck.

A few days earlier, on May 2, Nazi storm troopers had raided the offices of German trade unions. They had seized all union property and arrested union leaders. The unions were put under Nazi management.

Early on, Hitler had outlawed the Communist party. Now, on June 21, he dissolved the German Nationalist party, which had helped to bring him to power. The next day the Nazis outlawed the Social Democratic party of President von Hindenburg. The Nazis were now Germany's only political party. "It is a democratic fallacy that people want to govern themselves,"[10] Goebbels explained.

The Sterilization Program

On July 26, 1933, the Hitler government began a program to weed out Germans who did not measure up to the Nazi standard. These included adults and children who were "judged feebleminded, schizophrenic, epileptic, or alcoholic."[11] The selection was based on family history. Also at risk were those suffering from depression, deafness, blindness, or physical weakness.

All such people were to be sterilized—operated on so that they could not have children. Between the start of the program and the beginning of World War II, some 400,000 Germans were sterilized. In many cases the victims lost their desire for sex as well as their ability to have children.

Large-Scale Persecution Begins

In the summer of 1933 persecution of Jews and anti-Nazis got worse. Decrees and orders were issued by various levels of national, state, and local governments. These were enforced in helter-skelter fashion. Jewish lawyers—except for those who had served at the front during the war—were forbidden to practice. Jewish doctors were not allowed in certain hospitals, and over time they were restricted more and more. Jews were fired from government jobs, as well as from school and university posts.

Berlin's world-famous movie industry was taken over by the Nazis and turned into a tool for propaganda. Jews who had worked in film at many levels lost their jobs. Along with others who did not want to work under Nazi supervision, they fled Germany. Most went to Hollywood where they wrote, acted in, photographed, and directed many of the classic films of the time.

Some did not make it out of the country. They were caught in the early roundups of Jews and other anti-Nazis on made-up charges and sent to concentration camps. In August 1933 some 45,000 prisoners were being held in 65 such camps, the largest at Dachau. They were poorly fed and beaten regularly.

Hitler Pushes His Policies

On October 14, 1933, Hitler attacked the Treaty of Versailles. It must be broken, he said. Germany must rearm. He accused the nations of the world of treating Germany as a "second-class citizen"[12] and announced that Germany was leaving the League of Nations.

A few months later Hitler pushed through a piece of legislation known as the Law Regulating National Labor. It catered to the wealthy businessmen who had financed the Nazi party by holding down wages. It established that the "leader of the enterprise [employer] makes the decision for the employees and laborers" and declared that "the employees and laborers owe him faithfulness."[13]

To soften such antilabor policies, on March 21, 1934, Hitler announced a program to build a vast national highway system. Known as the *autobahn*, the system would join Germany's seaports and major cities and make shipping goods easier. When it was completed, it would also provide smooth driving for Germans in their new "people's cars" called *Volkswagens*. But most importantly, it would immediately create jobs for thousands of unemployed German workers.

Hitler also involved himself in foreign policy. In early June he traveled to Venice to meet with the dictator of Italy, Benito Mussolini, for the first time. The meeting would lead to a deadly alliance.

The Night of the Long Knives

Earlier in that month of June 1934, Hitler had met with Ernst Röhm. Rumors had reached Hitler that the SA leader was planning to join with Communists to topple the Nazi government. Röhm denied this and assured Hitler of his loyalty. Hitler didn't believe him. He claimed that Röhm was planning to "eliminate me personally."[14]

On June 30, Röhm and his lieutenants, some of them homosexual as was Röhm himself, were in their beds at an inn in Wannsee, not far from Munich. Around dawn a party of armed men led by Adolf Hitler burst into their quarters. Two of the men were dragged from the bed they shared and shot dead.

Ernst Röhm was seized, locked in a room with a loaded pistol, and told to kill himself. He refused. On Hitler's order, two henchmen then shot Röhm at point-blank range, killing him.

Meanwhile, back in Berlin, Göring and Himmler had led a group of SS men and special police in rounding up some 150 Nazi Brownshirt leaders. They were stood up against a wall and shot by a firing squad. Another squad of SS wearing civilian clothes killed former chancellor von Schleicher when he answered his doorbell. They also murdered his wife.

Members of the Brownshirts who were among those murdered in the Night of the Long Knives

Finally, Gregor Strasser, the Führer's most powerful rival, was seized at his home in Berlin. He was taken to the Gestapo jail and put in a cell. A few hours later he too was killed. Göring gave the order.

How many were killed altogether in the purge the Germans called the "Night of the Long Knives?"[15] Hitler's count was seventy-seven. Later information indicated that the correct figure was "more than 1,000."[16] Hitler justified the murders because, he said, those killed had been scheming with a foreign government to overthrow him. He also claimed that Röhm and others "deserved to die"[17] because of their "corrupt morals."[18]

The rank and file of the SA were now disarmed. Their duties were taken over by the Himmler SS. Among those duties was running the concentration camps. Himmler was now in charge of them and would remain so as they continued to expand both inside Germany and—after World War II began—beyond its borders.

Building Up the Army

A month after the Night of the Long Knives, the chancellor of Austria, Engelbert Dollfuss, was shot by Nazis in Vienna. They then held members of his cabinet hostage as they tried to work out a deal that would allow them to escape to Germany. The Nazis would not allow a doctor in to treat Dollfuss. He lay on the floor of his office for four hours, bleeding to death. Although they had been promised safe passage to Germany, the Nazis were arrested. When a mob tried to lynch them, martial law was declared and the Austrian army patrolled the streets of cities throughout the country. Kurt von Schussnigg then became chancellor of Austria. He would be a weak leader unable to stand up to either the Austrian Nazis or Hitler.

The eighty-five-year-old president of Germany, Paul von Hindenburg, died a few days after the Dollfuss murder. Hitler announced that his cabinet had merged the office of president with that of chancellor and that he would assume the leadership duties of both positions. He ordered that a vote be held for the German people to confirm him as the sole leader of the nation. On August 19, 1934, almost 90 percent of the voters approved Hitler as führer of Germany.

He was now commander in chief of the armed forces. The army had always been loyal to Hindenburg, who had led it during World War I, but now Hitler moved quickly to establish his authority over it. All officers and men of the armed forces were required to take an oath swearing "unconditional obedience to Adolf Hitler."[19]

Hitler bided his time until January 1935. That was when France and Germany had agreed that the people of the Saar, which France had held since the end of World War I, would vote on which country would rule them. The former German state lay along the Moselle River between the two countries. The vote was 477,000 to 48,000 in favor of rejoining Germany.

Now Hitler had the most coal-rich territory in Europe under his control. The Saar would provide the fuel he needed to increase production of arms and ammunition. Hitler could make weapons for his army. He could expand it. He announced a draft of German youth into the army.

The new law stated that Germany could be safe against an "arms-bristling Europe only through the rebirth of the German army."[20] Of course the draft was a serious violation of the Treaty of Versailles. This worried neither Hitler nor the German people nor the German press, which ran such headlines as "End of Versailles, Germany Free Again!"[21]

The Nuremberg Laws

Throughout 1935 "Free" Germany was becoming more and more of a nightmare for its Jewish citizens. In Berlin, Jews were set upon and viciously beaten by a gang of two hundred Nazis. In the Köln district Jews were forbidden to live within the boundaries of some towns. Buying from Jewish merchants was declared "treason to the people."[22] In Breslau, a group of twenty-four Jewish men and the non-Jewish girls they had dated were arrested, tried, found guilty of being "race defilers,"[23] and put in concentration camps.

On September 15, 1935, the so-called Nuremberg Laws were passed. They deprived Jews of German citizenship, prohibited marriage between Jews and Aryans, and forbid Jews to employ female servants under the age of thirty-five. Over the next few years the Nuremberg Laws would be expanded by thirteen decrees, making life in Germany more and more intolerable for Jews.

One young woman, Gretel Bergmann, was caught up in the web of laws. She was an athlete, a high jumper practicing to compete in the Olympic Games, which were going to be held in Berlin in 1936. She was also Jewish.

In 1935, twenty-one-year-old Gretel went to England and won the British women's high-jump championship. When she returned to Germany she was encouraged by Nazi sports officials to get ready for the Olympic trials. However, as a Jew she was denied membership in the German Athletic Association where the best training was possible. Even so, at the trials she tied the German record with a five-foot-three-inch high jump. Then, with the Olympics about to start, she received a letter from the German Olympic Committee telling her that as a Jew she would not be allowed to represent Germany in the Games. The letter was signed: "Heil Hitler!"[24]

Gretel managed to get out of Germany early in 1937. She made her way to the United States. In 1937 and 1938 she twice won the U.S. high-jump championship and also won the shot-put championship. In 1996 when she was asked about the Olympics being held in Atlanta, Georgia, she said she was "cheering for the Americans,"[25] not the German athletes from the land of her birth.

The Aggression Begins

While Berliners were preparing for the Olympic Games, Hitler again broke the Treaty of Versailles. This time he marched Germany's growing army to the west. The treaty had defined the lands bordering the Rhine River as a neutral zone between Germany and the countries to the west—France, the Netherlands, and Switzerland. Until 1930 the area, known as the Rhineland, had been occupied by troops of the victors of World War I. After 1930, it was supposed to be a demilitarized zone—an area off limits to troops of all nations.

On March 7, 1936, the German army occupied the Rhineland. The action brought the Krupp armaments factories and the I. G. Farben chemical works back under the German flag. Fueled by coal from the Saar, Krupp would turn out the tanks and cannons to bring Germany victory after victory at the start of World War II. Farben would supply the formula for the Zyklon-B crystals used to release the gas that killed millions in the concentration camps.

The troops in the Rhineland immediately began building the Siegfried Line—a series of cement bunkers, trenches, and fortifications, which were to be heavily armed with cannons and machine guns—along the western border of the Rhineland. Hitler called the invasion "the close of the struggle for German equality."[26]

Actually, it was the opening move in the Nazi conquest of Europe.

THE GATHERING STORM

6

 ehind the Nazi conquest of Europe was the principle of Lebensraum. Once this had meant getting back the lands lost by the Treaty of Versailles so that the German people would have enough room to live.

Under Adolf Hitler, however, Lebensraum had come to mean something quite different.

The Nazis believed that since the Germans were Aryans and therefore superior, they had a duty to reproduce in large numbers. German women were urged to have children. Young, unmarried Aryan women were encouraged to have babies out of wedlock with pure-blooded Nazis. Aryan population growth was a major aim of the Nazis.

Germany, even if its pre-World War I borders were restored, was not big enough to support such a growing population. There were not enough resources, farmland, or food. But there was much rich and fertile land in the countries to the east of Germany. There was iron ore, and oil, too. "This soil exists," wrote Hitler in *Mein Kampf*, "for the people which possesses the force to take it."[1]

The German people would grow. The inferior people would be enslaved or killed. There would be land and food and resources for Aryans. This was the Nazi dream. In speech after speech Hitler pushed his new definition of Lebensraum. And at the end of each speech the audience would shout "Heil Hitler!"

The Axis

Hitler was fanatic about Lebensraum, but he was quite practical in laying the groundwork to get it. If his armies moved east, Austria would be the first country in their path. There were many Austrian Nazis who would welcome them, many Austrians who—like Hitler himself—considered themselves Germans and Aryans. However, such a move would also bring him close to the Italian-Austrian border. It was important that the Italian dictator Mussolini not misunderstand the Austrian strategy.

There was also the future to consider. The Lebensraum Hitler wanted must come, he said, "largely at the expense of Russia."[2] (At that time, "Russia" generally referred to the larger Soviet Union, of which Russia was a part.) But to move toward Russia through countries like Czechoslovakia (today the Czech Republic and Slovakia) and Poland meant risking war with France and Britain, who were pledged to protect those countries' boundaries by the 1925 Pact of Locarno and other treaty obligations. Also, Russia was vast, extending all the way to the Sea of Japan, and Hitler did not want to stretch his army's supply lines that far. It would be helpful if some Russian armies were preoccupied with guarding those far regions against the possibility of a Japanese attack.

What all this added up to was that Hitler needed allies. He got them by the autumn of 1936, when Germany entered into a secret treaty with Italy, and then signed a mutual defense treaty with Japan. By this time Italy had already conquered Ethiopia, and Japan had invaded Manchuria (which bordered Russia) and China. The treaty ensured that the three nations would not interfere with one another's aggressions.

One of the pact's aims was to stop the spread of Russian communism in Europe and Asia. They called it an "anti-Communist Axis."[3] From then on, Germany, Italy, and Japan would be known collectively as the Axis.

A Big Lie

Less than a year after the Axis pact was signed, Hitler and Mussolini met in Nuremberg. The occasion was the giant September 1937 rally in which Hitler reviewed a parade of 800,000 soldiers and paratroopers. In keeping with Axis aims, there was also an anti-Communist exhibit.

The exhibit linked communism with the Jews. Julius Streicher, the whip-wielding publisher of *Der Sturmer*, was involved in it. He charged that the Jews were instructed by the Talmud—their sacred writings—that they had the right to kill non-Jews. (The Talmud says no such thing.) Streicher charged that this was the secret agenda of both Jewish Communists and capitalists.

Persecution of Jews in Germany was mounting. Increasing numbers of them were being sent to concentration camps. There were now four major camps in Germany—Dachau, Sachsenhausen, Lichtenburg, and Buchenwald—as well as many smaller camps. Besides Jews, they housed political prisoners, Gypsies, and homosexuals. Nazi logic held that "the Röhm revolt showed that sick people of this kind stick together"[4] and that all homosexuals were a danger to Germany. All of the prisoners at the four major concentration camps were starved, denied medical treatment, and forced to do hard labor. They were turned into living skeletons by the Himmler SS, which ran the camps.

The Austrian Anschluss

The first step in turning the SS into mass murderers was about to take place with the Austrian *Anschluss*. The word means a joining, or a formation of a union, and it had been a rallying cry for Nazis since the party began. By Anschluss they meant the "reunification"[5] of Germany with Austria, which had been a part of Germany in the tenth century, and had a German-speaking population. Such a union, although popular among many citizens in both countries, had been forbidden by the Treaty of Versailles.

Preparing for the Anschluss, which would involve moving German troops into Austria, on February 4, 1938, Hitler named himself supreme commander of the German armed forces. He also transferred control of foreign policy from the cabinet to himself, naming Göring and Hess as his new advisers. He forced two generals to retire for reasons having nothing to do with their military roles. The commander in chief of the army was accused of being homosexual and resigned. The field marshal who had served as war minister stepped down when his bride of one month was accused of being a former prostitute.

When they had been replaced by two new commanders on March 11, 1938, the German army moved into Austria. Austrian chancellor Schussnigg had tried in vain to work out compromises with both Hitler and the Austrian Nazis, but he was unable to stop the march toward Anschluss. Shortly after Hitler entered Vienna at the head of forty tanks, Schussnigg was arrested. He was held in custody by the Gestapo for seventeen months and then sent to the concentration camps of Sachsenhausen and Dachau. Somehow he survived the war.

There had been no opposition to the German invasion of Austria. On the contrary, most Austrians had greeted the Germans with cheers. Young girls had thrown flowers at them. Swastika flags were waved by children.

Hitler, however, didn't rely only on public displays of approval. He wanted the Anschluss to be legal in the eyes of the world. As the new führer of seventy million people, Austrians as well as Germans, he first named himself commander in chief of the armed forces of both countries, and saw to it that all Austrian soldiers took an oath to him personally. Then he called for a vote by the people of both Austria and Germany on Anschluss. It was held on April 10 and 99 percent of the voters in the two countries approved the union. The Austrians, it seemed, loved Hitler as much as the Germans did.

The Brown Bomber

A feeling was beginning to grow that with the combined German and Austrian armies at his disposal, Hitler could not be stopped. It seemed obvious that Czechoslovakia and Poland would be next in his hunger for Lebensraum. Like it or not, the Aryans seemed to be proving they had superiority when it came to military might.

But they weren't superior in all areas. One of the groups Hitler had called inferior in *Mein Kampf* was the black race. He considered that Max Schmeling, Germany's heavyweight champion boxer, had proven it when he took on the undefeated "Brown Bomber,"[6] Joe Louis, in 1936 and knocked out the African-American boxer from Detroit in the twelfth round.

Now, on June 22, 1938, there was a rematch. Louis came out of his corner in round one and knocked Schmeling down for a count of three. Schmeling got up and Louis knocked him down again, this time for a one-count. Back on his feet, Schmeling went down again, this time for good. His trainer threw in the towel at the count of five, ending the fight. Joe Louis had knocked out the pride of the Aryans in two minutes, four seconds of the first round. There was no joy in Nazi-land, but in America, blacks and whites, Jews and non-Jews, hailed Joe Louis as the hero who punched a hole straight through the middle of *Mein Kampf*.

Hitler accepted Schmeling's lie that he had been fouled by a kidney punch and turned his attention elsewhere. "Elsewhere" was the Sudetenland, that area of Czechoslovakia in which a German-speaking minority lived. Hitler threatened that if the Sudetenland was not given to Germany, he would "liberate"[7] it by force.

The president of Czechoslovakia, Edvard Beneš, knowing that his small country could not stand up against Hitler's army, asked other European nations for help. However, when a meeting was held in Munich to discuss the situation, he was barred from attending. Mussolini, Prime Minister Neville Chamberlain of Great Britain, and Premier Edouard Daladier of France met with Hitler to discuss the giveaway of Czechoslovakian territory. Czech officials were not asked to be present lest they raise embarrassing questions of national sovereignty and boundaries.

A peaceful agreement was arrived at. In order to prevent the war that he had threatened, Hitler could have the Sudetenland. In exchange, Hitler gave assurances that there would be no more aggression by Germany.

Hitler's arrival in Vienna, Austria, in March 1938

Prime Minister Chamberlain went back to London. He told the British people that with the Munich agreement he had ensured "peace in our time."[8] Not everybody believed that. Many thought that he had caved in to a bully with his policy of "appeasement"[9]—the word used to describe handing over the Sudetenland to avoid a fight.

The Germans marched into the Sudetenland on October 5, 1938. As in Austria, there was no opposition. Just as the Austrians had, the Sudeten Germans waved Nazi banners and threw flowers. Hitler "was treated as a hero"[10] when he entered the Sudeten city of Eger.

The Night of Broken Glass

Meanwhile, back in Germany the constant anti-Semitic propaganda and harassment of Jews was reaching a boiling point. It exploded following the killing of a member of the German Embassy in Paris by a teenaged Polish Jew. The youth said his act was to avenge the treatment of his parents in Germany. His father had been one of ten thousand Jews shipped to Poland in boxcars by the Nazis.

Propaganda chief Goebbels saw the crime as a perfect excuse for widespread "spontaneous demonstrations"[11] against Jews throughout Germany. But, of course, these demonstrations weren't spontaneous. They were organized by Reinhard Heydrich, the number two man in the SS whom Himmler had put in charge of the Gestapo.

"Hangman Heydrich," as he would later be known, had been thrown out of the German navy at the age of twenty-six for sexual misconduct with a woman. Under Himmler, he had organized a network of spies, informers, and thugs throughout Germany. Now Heydrich put this entire network to work all at once. The result was *Kristallnacht*—the Night of Broken Glass.

It was called that because the glass windows and doors of about 7,500 Jewish shops and businesses were smashed during the night of November 9 and early morning of November 10, 1938. Over eight hundred of these were completely destroyed. Also destroyed were 191 synagogues, most of which were burned to the ground.

Hundreds of Jewish homes were broken into and ransacked. Some were set afire. Some Jewish women were raped. More than ninety Jews were killed. Thirty thousand Jews—mostly men—were arrested and shipped to concentration camps.

The property damage added up to hundreds of millions of dollars. Much of what was destroyed were goods that Jewish merchants did not own, but rather put on their shelves with the understanding that their non-Jewish manufacturers would be paid for them after the goods were sold. Along with the Jewish store owners, these non-Jewish suppliers filed claims for damages with the insurance companies responsible for covering their losses.

When Göring learned from Heydrich that non-Jewish property had been destroyed, he was furious. "I wished you had killed two hundred Jews instead of destroying such valuables!"[12] he roared. Then he came up with a partial solution for the insurance companies.

Göring gave them the right to deny the claims filed by Jews. He pointed out to them that this would save them a fortune. "I should like to go fifty-fifty with you,"[13] he added greedily.

Laughing Into the Grave

Germany, Hitler realized, had been disgraced in the eyes of the world by Kristallnacht. Göring was ordered to do something about it. The Jews would have to be disposed of in a more orderly way. In response, Göring set up the Reich Center for Jewish Emigration under the SS. It would be run by Adolf Eichmann.

Eichmann was an Austrian born in the same part of the country as Hitler. He had joined the Nazi party early, been involved in an attempt to overthrow the pre-Nazi Austrian government, and fled to Germany in 1934. Here he had joined the SS and by 1938 had established himself as an expert on Jewish affairs.

Eichmann's new job at first involved getting Jews to leave Germany and Austria in large numbers while leaving their property behind in Nazi hands. Later that would change, and his main work would be arranging and scheduling the transportation of millions of Jews to the concentration camps where they would be gassed to death. Another Nazi who worked with Eichmann later testified that he had said "he would leap laughing into the grave because the feeling that he had five million people on his conscience would be for him a source of extraordinary satisfaction."[14]

The First Double Cross

Even before the mass murders of World War II, Eichmann and the Reich Center for Jewish Emigration became involved in the fate of the Jews of other countries. On March 15, 1939, Hitler broke the promise he made to Chamberlain at Munich and the German army occupied the rest of Czechoslovakia. An exception was a small area of Slovakia invaded by Hungarian troops under orders from a pro-Nazi Hungarian government friendly to Hitler.

When Hitler entered the Czech capital city of Prague, however, he was not greeted with swastika flags and flowers as he had been in Vienna and the Sudetenland. In most of Czechoslovakia, the people were Slavs, not Germans or Aryans. He was met with silence and occasional boos. The Czechs were fearful, particularly those who were Jewish.

They had good reason. In the Czech area of Slovakia alone, some 17,000 Jews would be rounded up and deported to Poland by authority of Adolf Eichmann and the Reich Center for Jewish Emigration. Later, Slovakian government officials made inquiries about them to the SS. The officials asked for permission to visit the Slovakian Jews. Adolf Eichmann replied that "such a visit was impossible. The Jews were dead."[15]

The Second Double Cross

Hitler had broken his word by taking over Czechoslovakia. He had clearly shown that his drive for Lebensraum was not over. Yet the French and the British, who had dealt with him at Munich, did not act.

In May 1939, Germany and Italy signed a "Pact of Steel."[16] Hitler and Mussolini agreed that "Germany would rule on land and Italy on sea in times of war."[17] Their choice of words was obviously a threat. Still France and Britain did not move.

Now the unthinkable happened. On August 23, Nazi Germany and Communist Russia signed a nonaggression pact. Hitler, who had built his career on opposing communism, and who in 1936 had united Germany with Italy and Japan in an Axis designed to keep Russian communism from spreading, had cut a deal with the Communist Russian dictator, Joseph Stalin. Given the untrustworthiness of the two leaders, it was inevitable that the alliance would end in betrayal.

In 1939, however, the French and British governments were stunned by the pact. Even though they had been alarmed by Nazism, they had always regarded it as a safeguard against Russian communism. That was one reason why they had dealt gently with Hitler. Now that reason was gone. Hitler had duped them again. They were very worried and stepped up arms production and defense measures.

World War II Begins

One week after the pact with Russia was signed, on September 1, 1939, one and a quarter million Nazi troops stormed across the Polish border. Almost one thousand tanks backed them up. German dive bombers attacked the Polish capital city of Warsaw. Fifteen days later, Russian troops invaded Poland from the east. Sixty thousand Poles died in the initial invasion, 200,000 were wounded, and 700,000 Polish soldiers were taken prisoner.

France and Britain had been pledged to defend Poland if the country was attacked. Now they sent Hitler a message saying that if he didn't withdraw from Poland, it meant war. Hitler ignored the threat. At last Britain and France acted. They declared war on Germany.

World War II had begun. Before it was over, sixty million lives would be lost.

7 THE FALL OF

EUROPE

ust as the war started in September 1939, Hitler ordered that all hospital and asylum mental patients who could not be cured should be put to death. This would mean a savings of money and manpower, which could then be used to fight the war. About 100,000 people, almost all of them Germans, were killed by technicians, nurses, doctors, and psychiatrists.

That same month, Reinhard Heydrich issued the directive forcing Polish Jews to live in ghettoes. "The concentration of the Jews from the countryside in the larger cities" was necessary to achieve the "final goal."[1] The final goal was understood by those carrying out Heydrich's order to mean that the Jews would be killed.

On October 18, 1939, German and Russian troops, which had invaded separate areas of Poland, met and Poland was defeated. The rounding up and transporting of Polish Jews began soon after. It took place during the severe winter of 1939–1940 in temperatures forty degrees below zero. Babies, children, the old, and the ill died by the thousands from cold and hunger. Many who could not keep up were left to die. Some were shot by their German guards because they were delaying the operation.

Many of those who made it to the ghettoes were ill with diseases brought on by their ordeal. Overcrowding in the ghettoes caused unsanitary conditions. Diseases like tuberculosis and typhoid spread quickly. To prevent them spreading further, walls were built and guards were posted to keep the Jews inside the ghettoes.

At the beginning of the war, "about 3,350,000, or 10 percent, of Poland's inhabitants"[2] were Jewish. Mostly the Jews lived in cities and towns, and mostly they were self-employed, or employed by fellow Jews. A history of laws against Jews, and of pogroms—anti-Jewish riots marked by robbery, rape, and random murder—had discouraged most Jews from becoming a part of Polish community life. The attitudes of pre-World War II Poles toward them "ranged from tolerance to animosity."[3]

In small towns and cities Jewish merchants had given credit to peasant and working-class customers. The Nazis canceled these debts. When Jews were forced to move to the ghettoes, Poles were able to move into their apartments and houses. Poles often took over the businesses and property the Jews left behind.

Nevertheless, while many Poles were being shipped to Germany as slave labor, the Jews were kept in Poland. Some Poles believed the Nazis were favoring the Jews. Some cooperated with the Nazi persecution of the Jews.

This was not true, however, of all Poles. A Polish organization called *Zegota* formed a Council for Aid to Jews. Its members found hiding places for Jews, prepared false documents for them, placed Jewish children in Catholic orphanages, brought in Polish doctors to treat Jews who became ill in hiding, and donated money to help Jews escape. While some of the Polish underground groups who kept on fighting the Nazis after the country surrendered were anti-Semitic, others supplied arms and ammunition to Jewish fighters in the ghetto and fought alongside them. Individual Poles risked their lives to hide Jews and help them in other ways.

Blitzkrieg!

The Nazis used the word *blitzkrieg* to describe the speed and fury of the drive to conquer Poland. Blitzkrieg does not, however, describe Germany's march west. On October 17, 100,000 German troops attacked France. On December 12 the Nazis poured more troops into an offensive along the Rhine. However, the

A group of Jewish men are rounded up and marched down a street in Cracow, Poland, in 1939.

Germans did not push the offensive because Hitler was hoping to arrange peace terms with the British. Nor did the French and British counterattack. There followed the period known as the Phony War, which ended on May 10, 1940.

On April 9, 1940, Germany had launched another blitzkrieg, this one against Denmark. Nazi forces occupied the capital city of Copenhagen. However, the real goal was neighboring Norway, which Germany would use as a base for attacks on shipping in the North Sea. Norway, realizing it was next on the Nazis' hit list, immediately declared war on Germany.

Meanwhile, the French and British had been reinforced by 90,000 Jews from Palestine. The Germans couldn't risk a direct attack. Instead, the Nazis launched a blitzkrieg on three small neutral nations—Holland, Belgium, and Luxembourg—in order to attack from a different direction. Nazi tank battalions descended on France from the northeast. Holland surrendered on May 25, followed three days later by Belgium.

The French army was now in full retreat. The British—340,000 troops—were trapped at Dunkirk on the French coast. The British navy, aided by fishing boats, pleasure yachts, and other private vessels, managed to rescue them before the Nazis could force their surrender. With the Germans victorious, Italy declared war on France and Britain. The Nazis occupied Paris. The victory was complete when the Norwegian army surrendered on June 10.

Occupied Western Europe

By June 1940 the Germans occupied the Netherlands, Belgium, Luxembourg, Denmark, Norway, Czechoslovakia, and Poland. German allies in Europe included Italy, Bulgaria, Romania, and Hungary. Most of the occupied countries and Nazi allies passed anti-Jewish laws and enforced them. Now not just Germany and Austria, but all of Europe was to be Judenrein.

The Nazis occupied northern France and set up a puppet French government for southern France in Vichy. One of the Vichy government's first acts was to create a Commissariat of Jewish Affairs. The commissariat took away the citizenship of French Jews who hadn't been born in France. A few months later it barred all Jews from working in the French civil service, and from management positions in industry and media. Jewish officers were dismissed from the French army.

The Jewish population of France had been greatly increased by refugees fleeing the Nazis. Eventually the commissariat would oversee the roundup of non-French Jews for shipment to death camps. In both Vichy France and occupied France, including Paris, the French police would conduct these roundups.

In Norway the Nazis put Vidkun Quisling in charge of the government. There were 1,700 Jews in the country, most of them refugees from the Nazis. Quisling's newly established police force managed to turn over half of them to the Nazis.

The Belgian police, however, refused to cooperate with the roundup of Jews. Belgian railroad employees sabotaged trains transporting Jews, left boxcar doors unlocked, and staged ambushes so that the Jews could escape. Most of the Belgian Jews had fled the country when the Nazis invaded. Of the 50,000 Jews who were left, only 5,000 had been born in Belgium. Some 25,000 Jews in Belgium would survive the war.

The Netherlands was different. Dutch police rounded up refugee Jews and Dutch Jews alike. In Amsterdam, the police chief, Sybren Tulp, was so enthusiastic that the city did indeed become Judenrein. Among the Amsterdam Jews shipped to the camps would be Anne Frank, the Jewish teenager whose diary still reminds us that even in the midst of mass murder there can be hope.

The Heroic Danes

There is hope, too, in the story of Nazi-occupied Denmark. "The behavior of the Danish people and their government," writes historian Hannah Arendt, "was unique among all the countries of Europe."[4] They refused to endorse anti-Semitism.

The Nazis said that Jews must wear a yellow badge with a star on it to identify them as Jews. The Danish government replied that the non-Jewish king of Denmark would be the first to wear the badge. They also told the Nazis that the members of the government would all resign rather than enforce anti-Jewish measures; nor would they cooperate in separating the 1,400 German Jewish refugees in Denmark from the 6,400 Danish Jews.

Despite lack of Danish cooperation, the Nazis decided to round up the Jews in Denmark. The Danish government learned about the plan. Danish civilians were organized to hide the Jews. Danish fishing boats spent almost a month ferrying 5,919 Jews out of the country to neutral Sweden, which granted them a haven from the Nazis. Almost all the rest of the Danish Jews survived the war in hiding in Denmark.

The German police had managed to arrest only a few hundred Danish Jews, most of them old people who were shipped to the Theresienstadt ghetto in Czechoslovakia. However, Danish officials made such a fuss about them by making constant inquiries as to their health and living conditions that most of them survived the war. Of the forty-eight who didn't, most died of old age.

Central European Anti-Semitism

In Romania the story was different. There were many more Jews in central and Eastern Europe than in the west. There were 750,000 Jews living in Romania in December 1940, when the pro-Nazi Iron Guard took over the Romanian government. General Ion Antonescu became the dictator of Romania.

Not long afterward, an anti-Semitic riot in the city of Iasa left several thousand Jews dead. Antonescu then ordered a roundup of Jews in the regions across the Dniester River. Tens of thousands of them were killed. Later, Romanian troops would conduct the largest massacre of Jews in Europe outside of the death camps.

By contrast, in Bulgaria all of the pressure that the Nazis brought to make the country Judenrein had little effect. Their Bulgarian allies had no "understanding of the Jewish problem."[5] When Jews were forced to wear the yellow badge with the star, there was so much "sympathy from the misled population," a German Nazi official observed, "that they actually are proud of their sign."[6] The Nazis became convinced that the Bulgarian king Boris was protecting the Jews, so they killed him. Despite the murder, not a single Bulgarian Jew was sent to the death camps, and none died at the hands of the Nazis.

In Hungary, non-Hungarian Jews were delivered to the Nazis early in the war. Land owned by Jews was taken over by the pro-Nazi government. In rural areas there were widespread pogroms. Hungarian volunteers fought alongside the Germans on the Eastern front and helped round up and kill the Jews of Eastern Europe. Out of a Hungarian Jewish population of 800,000, only 160,000 would survive the war.

Greece, Yugoslavia, and Italy

In April 1941 the German army invaded Yugoslavia (today Croatia and Bosnia), took over the capital city of Belgrade, and occupied the country. In the Serbian areas of Yugoslavia, the Nazi occupying army was under constant attack from Serb guerrilla fighters. To strike back, the Nazis took hostages and shot them. They also shot and killed almost the entire male Jewish population. Jewish women and children, along with Gypsies, were put to death by poison gas.

In the Croatian part of Yugoslavia, the Nazis set up a puppet government. The Croats were much more pro-Nazi and anti-Semitic than the Serbs. "Croatia killed almost half of its Jewish population in its own annihilation camps," according to Holocaust historian Raul Hilberg. In addition, 30,000 Croatian Jews were sent to the Nazi death camps.

Back in October 1940, the Nazis' Italian allies had invaded Greece. When the Greek army fought them off, the Germans had come to the aid of the Italians. Now, shortly after the Yugoslavian invasion, the Germans captured the Greek capital of Athens and the Greek army surrendered.

Two thirds of the Jews of Greece—about 55,000 people—lived in Salonika. With the German takeover, they were herded into a ghetto. Within two months they had all been shipped to concentration camps.

Some Greek Jews managed to escape to that area of Greece that was under Italian control. Here they were safe until the end of the war when the Italian army collapsed and the Germans took over. Thirteen thousand of them were then sent to their deaths.

The Italians, under pressure from their German Nazi allies, had passed anti-Semitic laws. However, they enforced them very weakly in Italy and in some of the areas they occupied, like Greece, not at all. Rather than kill their Jews, the Italians "put them instead into Italian camps where they were quite safe until the Germans occupied the country"[7] toward the end of the war. As a result, more than 90 percent of Italy's Jews survived the Holocaust.

Operation Barbarossa

In the early days of the war, while Adolf Hitler's murderous policies were starting to be carried out, Hitler himself was occupied with secret plans for Operation Barbarossa. This was the Nazi name for an invasion of Russia in violation of the nonaggression pact between the two countries. Hitler's purpose was to take from Russia the Lebensraum he had promised the German people.

On June 22, 1941, German forces attacked Russia. The Nazi army, along with the Finns and the Romanians, who supported the invasion, numbered 8.95 million troops. The Russian army numbered 7.15 million soldiers. The battles that followed would be the most costly in history in terms of human life.

For the Jews, who had already been through so much, it would be the worst of times. One month after the Russian invasion, in July 1941, Reich marshal Hermann Göring issued the order for the "final solution of the Jewish question."[8]

8
THE
FINAL
SOLUTION

"I n mid-March 1942 some 75 to 80 percent of all victims of the Holocaust were still alive, while 20 to 25 percent had perished," observes Holocaust historian Professor Christopher R. Browning. "A mere eleven months later, in mid-February 1943, the percentages were exactly the reverse."[1]

Roughly one million Jews had already been murdered between the issuing of the final solution order in July 1941 and mid-March 1942. Most of them were killed in Poland, the Ukraine, Latvia, Estonia, Lithuania, and western Russia. These were the battle zones of the German-Russian war. Some of the Jewish civilians who died were casualties of battles. The overwhelming majority were not. They were murdered by squads, which had been organized for the purpose of killing them.

The first such killing squads were called *Einsatzgruppen* and were made up of four SS units. SS chief Heinrich Himmler had assigned each unit an area the German army had taken from the Russians in its initial Operation Barbarossa blitzkrieg. Their job was to secure the conquered areas. Himmler's deputy, Reinhard Heydrich, explained to the Einsatzgruppen officers that this meant "that all Jews were supposed to be exterminated without regard to age or sex."[2]

The Einsatzgruppen were made up of about three thousand men. This was simply not enough manpower to secure German-occupied Eastern Europe. Three more SS brigades totalling 25,000 men and 38 battalions of Order Police were sent to help the Einsatzgruppen.

The Order Police—19,000 men and officers who were frequently rotated so that perhaps three times that number served beside the SS in Eastern Europe—were drawn from the reserve police units of large German cities, and from civil servants and other civilians not considered fit for army duty. They were older men, often married and with families. Later their ranks were swelled by young recruits. Most Order Police were not members of the Nazi party. They were assigned to perform police duties in occupied areas. However, when this turned out to mean rounding up and killing Jewish men, women, and children, few of them hesitated to obey.

At first only Jewish men were killed, the excuse being that they were Communists. Then, on August 1, 1941, Himmler issued this order: "All Jews must be shot; Jewish women are to be driven into the swamps."[3] The second part of the order, which applied to children as well as women, was meant to keep their slaughter as secret as possible.

The Bialystok Massacre

Only a few days after Operation Barbarossa began, Police Battalion 309 entered the captured Polish city of Bialystok. Ordered to round up the Jews, they began shooting them at random. A survivor remembers that "the shooting lasted the entire day."[4] The gutters piled up with dead bodies.

Finally some seven hundred Jews were forced into the Bialystok synagogue, the largest synagogue in Poland. The building was locked. It was doused with gasoline and set afire. The Germans shot those who tried to escape. The others burned to death. Between 2,000 and 2,200 Jews died in Bialystok that day.

In July 1940, Russian troops had occupied Lithuania and deported large numbers of the population regarded as opponents to communism. Now, shortly before Bialystok and two days after advance units of the German army liberated Lithuania from the Russians, there was a pogrom in the capital city of Kaunas. Several thousand Jews were murdered by Lithuanians. Those Jews left in Kaunas and those in other Lithuanian cities were herded into ghettoes.

In July 1941, in the Vilnius region, 1,150 Lithuanians were employed by a German Einsatzgruppen unit to help round up and shoot five hundred Jews a day. On September 19 another Einsatzgruppen unit recorded that 42,692 people—most of them Jews—had been shot with the help of Lithuanian squads. Volunteer Lithuanian killing units functioned as far as 800 miles (1,287 kilometers) from the Lithuanian border.

In Lithuania, Latvia, and Estonia, the Germans were greeted as rescuers from Soviet Russian tyranny. The police in all three countries worked with the German Order Police in rounding up and killing Jews. Often they helped in killing operations beyond their countries' borders.

Estonia had a population of little more than a million, only four thousand of them Jews. The German Einsatzgruppen, helped by Estonian volunteers, shot 440 Jewish men. The rest of the Jews were shipped out of Estonia to German-held territory in Russia where they were killed. Later, when one thousand Jews were shipped from the Theresienstadt camp in Czechoslovakia to Estonia, the Estonian Security Police lined them up and shot them.

There were 70,000 Jews in Latvia when the German army swept through that country. Four months later, 30,000 of them had been killed by German and Latvian police forces. Another 27,800 Jews who had been squeezed into the ghetto of the Latvian capital city of Riga were killed in November and December. More than 100,000 Latvians enlisted in the German army. Many took part in the killing of Jews in Poland, the Ukraine, and Russia.

Babi Yar

Non-German units that worked under the German Order Police in killing Jews and performing other tasks were called *Schutzmannschaft*. They were organized into battalions each five hundred strong. They were moved wherever they were needed in German-held territory.

Early in the war the largest section of Russia under German control was the Ukraine. It had a population of 36 million people. They had lived unwillingly

SS guards stand in formation outside the commandant's house in the
Belzec death camp in Poland.

under both Russian and Polish rule. Almost three million Jews lived in the Ukraine, which had a long history of pogroms. The Nazis considered the Ukrainians inferior and the Ukrainians considered the Jews inferior. To the Nazis, this made the Ukrainians ideal Schutzmannschaft. Eighteen and a half Ukrainian Schutzmannschaft battalions were organized in the year following the German invasion of Russia.

Throughout the war the Ukrainian Schutzmannschaft would be used to round up and kill Jews, and also as concentration camp guards. In the early days they would often get drunk before performing mass killings. They functioned in Poland and other sections of Russia, as well as in the Ukraine itself.

In late September 1941 a German police battalion and a western Ukrainian Schutzmannschaft battalion came to a place called Babi Yar on the outskirts of the city of Kiev in the central Ukraine. They rounded up the Jews—men, women, and children alike—marched them in small groups to the edge of a ravine, and mowed them down with machine guns. The dead bodies fell backward into the ravine.

It went on for two days. When it was over, 33,000 Jews were dead. Most had been killed by Ukrainians.

The Gas Vans

The shooting of Jews by Germans, or under German supervision, was going on throughout Eastern Europe in 1941 and 1942. But killing people by machine gun or rifle fire was too slow a process for the Nazis. It wasn't efficient. It was feared that the ongoing killing of unarmed civilians might harm morale. Other ways of killing were considered.

As early as September 1941, explosives were tested as a means of killing mentally ill people in the occupied Russian city of Minsk. Twenty-five of them were locked in bunkers and an explosion was set off. The results were messy, so the Nazis ruled out the use of explosives.

On September 3 the gas produced by Zyklon-B crystals was tested in the Auschwitz concentration camp for the first time. (Zyklon-B, amethyst-blue crystals of hydrogen cyanide, had originally been sold commercially as a strong disinfectant.) The victims were Russian soldiers who had been taken prisoner, which was against the rules of war. Rudolf Hess, the commandant of Auschwitz, witnessed the killing and was satisfied. "Now we had the gas," he said, "and we had established a procedure."[5] What the Nazis lacked, however, were large gas chambers.

A different test was conducted at a mental asylum. This time twenty to thirty patients were locked in a sealed room with two pipes driven into the walls. A car was parked outside and its exhaust pipe was attached to one of the pipes. The car's engine was turned on and carbon monoxide began seeping into the room. When another car was hooked up to the second pipe, death followed.

This sparked the idea for "killing vans." These were trucks with sealed compartments and they came in two sizes. The larger vans could hold between 130 and 150 victims. The smaller ones held 80 to 100. Carbon monoxide was pumped into the compartments by a tube leading from the exhaust pipe. The killing process took between fifteen and thirty minutes.

The gas vans were manufactured by the Gabschat Farengewerke of Berlin. The first ones were used in the Chelmno death camps at the end of 1941. They were also supplied to the Einsatzgruppen to dispose of the Jews rounded up by them and their helpers.

At Chelmno, where the vans remained stationary, they were found to be satisfactory. But in Einsatzgruppen operations where the vans had to be mobile, there were problems. Often the connections didn't hold properly. And if they did, what was to be done with the bodies? There were no ovens to burn them as there would be at permanent death camps.

The vans had not solved the problem. The Jews were not being killed quickly enough. In January 1942 a conference was held at Wannsee, a suburb of Berlin, to decide how to move the final solution along more efficiently.

As a result of this conference, industry, transportation networks, army and police units in Germany and other countries would join together to kill the millions of European Jews still alive in mid-March 1942. It would be the largest mass killing in history. It would be genocide—the all-out campaign to wipe out an entire people.

9
THE DEATH CAMPS

he month before the Wannsee Conference, in December 1941, the Japanese bombed the U.S. Navy fleet at Pearl Harbor and the United States declared war on Japan. Four days later the U.S. declared war on Japan's Axis partners, Germany and Italy. Two days before Pearl Harbor, on December 5, the advance of the German army to within 20 miles (32 kilometers) of the Russian capital city of Moscow had been halted by a counterattack. The rest of the German army in Russia was spread thin. One part was advancing in the Crimea, while another was bogged down in the fierce fighting that was part of the siege of Leningrad, Russia's second-largest city. Therefore, the German troops in Moscow could not be reinforced. A harsh winter was upon them, and for the first time in the Russian campaign the German troops had to fall back.

With a new enemy and fierce Russian resistance, the war should have been the Nazis' first concern. However, it often wasn't. The Wannsee Conference set up a different priority: "The Jews have to disappear"[1] was how it was defined at the conference by Hans Frank, the Nazi governor-general of the general government of Poland.

The general government of Poland consisted of the western regions that Germany had first conquered in 1939. It included Warsaw, Cracow, Lublin, Lvov, and Radom. Its Jewish population was about 2,284,000. The conference approved the suggestion that these Polish Jews be "destroyed first."[2]

Named after the number two man in the SS, Reinhard Heydrich, the mass murder of the Polish Jews would be called "Operation Reinhard" by the Nazis. Known as the "Hangman of Europe,"[3] Heydrich was killed on June 10, 1942, near the village of Lidice by Czech guerrilla fighters. For revenge, the Nazis destroyed the village and murdered the 1,300 civilians who lived there.

The first steps in Operation Reinhard had been taken long before his death. Those Jews not killed in the mass shootings had been herded into ghettoes. The Lublin district of Poland was declared "a Jewish reservation,"[4] and the Nazis resettled tens of thousands of Jews from Germany, Austria, and Slovakia there. Many of them were used as slave labor in clothing factories set up by the SS in Lublin.

It was then decided that the Lublin district should be treated as Lebensraum and that Germans should resettle there and build up its industry. The Jews would provide the slave labor. The SS would oversee this project. The Jewish slaves, however, would not live among the resettled Germans. A concentration camp was built to house the 50,000 prisoners who would work in the new enterprises under German supervision. The camp was called Madjanek.

Madjanek was used not only to house Jews, but Russian prisoners of war who were also used as slave labor. There is no record of how many Russians and Jews died at Madjanek. However, in only one day near the end of the war, 18,000 Jews were killed there.

The Commandant of Auschwitz

Madjanek was a minor cog in Operation Reinhard. Auschwitz, not far from the city of Cracow, was the most effective death camp. The commandant of Auschwitz was Rudolf Hess, and he took his job very seriously.

Hess had joined the Nazi party in 1922. The next year he was sentenced to life in prison by a German court for murdering a Jew. He was released in 1928 and joined the SS. He rose in its ranks to oversee Auschwitz.

"I was ordered to establish extermination facilities at Auschwitz in June 1941,"[5] he wrote. After testing other chemicals, he decided that the gas produced by Zyklon-B, which "took from three to fifteen minutes to kill,"[6] would be most efficient. "We built our gas chambers to accommodate two thousand people at one time whereas at Treblinka their ten gas chambers only accommodated two hundred people each,"[7] he boasted. Auschwitz would have four such chambers, as well as furnaces to burn the bodies.

Two tons of Zyklon-B crystals a month were supplied by Tesch and Stabenow, a Hamburg company. They put in a bid to supply ventilating and heating equipment for the gas chambers, as well. There were also bills from the Desau firm of Degesch for three quarters of a ton of cyanide crystals a month.

I. A. Topf and Sons, a heating equipment manufacturing company located in Erfurt, was awarded the contract to build the ovens for burning the bodies at Auschwitz. Their letter of acceptance said: "We acknowledge receipt of your order for five triple furnaces, including two electric elevators for raising the corpses and one emergency elevator."[8] Another company seeking the contract wrote that "for putting the bodies into the furnace, we suggest simply a metal fork moving on cylinders."[9]

Before they were killed, the more able-bodied victims worked. "Such famous German firms as I. G. Farben, the Krupp Werke, and Siemens-Schuckert Werke had established plants in Auschwitz as well as near the Lublin death camps,"[10] reported Hannah Arendt, who covered the trial of Nazi Adolf Eichmann. After they were killed, gold fillings were pulled from the victims' teeth, melted down, and shipped to a bank where the gold was deposited to a secret SS account under the name Max Heliger.

Most of the Jews who were herded into ghettoes before being shipped to death camps had believed they were going to be resettled in some better place when they were moved this second time. They had been urged to bring whatever jewelry they owned with them. They also brought whatever money they had. After their deaths, the money and the valuables were also deposited in the Max Heliger account.

Children behind barbed wire at Auschwitz

The Death Trains

Although Polish Jews were the first target of Operation Reinhard, other Jews were shipped from all over Europe to the death camps. Hundreds of thousands were jammed into boxcars for "resettlement." Death trains moving from west to east clogged the railway lines. They rolled from 1942 through 1945, a period during which Germany was locked in a death struggle with Russia and losing. The railroads were desperately needed to carry supplies to German armies in the east. But the death trains were the first priority.

The overall planning and supervision of the death trains was the job of SS *Obersturmbannfuhrer* (Lieutenant Colonel) Adolf Eichmann, the Gestapo specialist in charge of the Reich Center for Jewish Emigration. Eichmann and his aides traveled throughout the conquered countries to secure cooperation from local authorities in rounding up their Jewish populations and loading them onto the death trains. They also worked closely with those who ran the railroads in the countries through which the trains moved to make sure the rail lines were kept clear for their passage. Sometimes supply trains were shunted aside. Other times unheated boxcars jammed with suffering human cargo sat on sidings in the bitter cold for hours, even days, while supplies were moved to the front. Many of those in the boxcars died.

Eichmann worked with people like the Austrian Hanns Rauter, who sent 100,000 of the 140,000 Jews in the Netherlands to the death camps—the highest percentage in Western Europe. Major General Otto Kohl, in charge of the railroads of Belgium and France, volunteered to supply Eichmann with trains for the death camps. In France the police rounded up Jewish children. About 12 percent of the death-train Jews from France were under the age of fifteen. Almost 20 percent of those from Belgium were also that young. There are no figures available for the many children shipped to the death camps from the other countries of Europe.

The boxcars of prisoners were unloaded at railroad sidings away from the main buildings at death camps like Auschwitz. Here the prisoners were sorted out by SS doctors and it was decided who was fit to be put to work in one of the camp factories and who would go immediately to the gas chambers. Old people, children, pregnant women, the ill, and the disabled would be led off to buildings edged by flower beds with signs over the entrances reading "Baths."[11] Waltzes and other pleasant music would be played as the prisoners were marched toward these buildings.

They would be separated by sex and made to undress outside the buildings. Inside they would see showerheads in the ceilings of the large chambers. Some of these people had been in the boxcars for as long as a week. Few things were as welcome to them as a shower. The doors were sealed behind them and the Zyklon-B crystals were dropped, releasing the poison gas.

Some of these procedures had been passed along from Hitler's 1939 "euthanasia program"[12]—the killing of incurable mental patients. About one hundred of the medical personnel who took part in that program helped arrange the killings at the death camps. Thousands of others were also involved in the death-camp killings. At Auschwitz alone Hess estimated that he "had a staff of approximately three thousand men" with which "to kill two thousand persons a day."[13]

These men, however, did not do the cleanup work. That was left to the *Sonderkommandos*—male Jewish prisoners who were given enough food and allowed to live in exchange for handling the bodies, removing the gold fillings from teeth, and stacking the corpses for the furnaces. Periodically, the Sonderkommandos would be killed and others assigned to take their places. At the Treblinka concentration camp in 1945, it was the Sonderkommandos who led an armed rebellion against the guards.

Operation Erntefest

The uprising in Treblinka, along with another at the Sobibor camp, shook up the Nazis. They had fought pitched battles with the Jews in ghettoes, including a three-week struggle to round up those in the Warsaw ghetto and deport them to death camps. But they had kept the Jewish prisoners in the camps weak from exposure and lack of food so that they would have no strength to rebel. Now the Nazis were worried. Also, they were losing the war in Poland and Russian troops were advancing on the eastern camps. There were 45,000 to 50,000 Jews in the labor camps in the Lubin district alone and they posed a real danger of organized rebellion as news of the death camps circulated among them.

Himmler decided that it was more important to kill these Jews than to use them for slave labor. That was the start of Operation *Erntefest* (Harvest Festival). It began at the Poniatowa labor camp where some 15,000 Jewish men, women, and children worked for the Walther C. Tobbens clothing company. All were shot and killed by a police unit of between 1,000 and 1,500 men.

The SS killed between 8,000 and 10,000 more at the Trawniki camp. At Madjenek, 18,000 were killed. In all, 42,000 Jews were murdered during Operation *Erntefest*.

The End of the War

By the end of 1944, the war was drawing to a close. The German army was being decimated by lack of supplies, starvation, and exposure throughout the cruel winter. By spring they were in full retreat from the advancing Russian armies. With the addition of fresh U.S. troops, the Allied forces had overcome the German counterattack known as the Battle of the Bulge, driven the Germans from France and Belgium, and were now penetrating deep into Germany.

Adolf Hitler had almost been killed by a bomb in a plot organized by top German generals alarmed at the unrealistic demands he was making of their forces. Now Hitler was giving orders directly to his armies, demanding that they not retreat, that they stand and die, that they ignore their lack of food, warm clothing, shoes, and other necessities. Naval blockades and Allied military actions had cut supply lines to the German civilian population as well. By spring 1945, two million Germans were refugees, fleeing aerial bombardments, artillery shellings, and the harsh reprisals being taken by the advancing Russians.

Incredibly, there was a frenzy of gassing at some of the camps to kill the Jewish prisoners while there was still time. Other camps, Auschwitz among them, were evacuated and the prisoners were made to march westward under guard. These were the death marches.

The prisoners were already weak from hunger and sick from exposure, and the forced marches made them weaker. Many fell by the wayside and died from the cold. Others, unable to keep up, were shot by their guards. Finally, large numbers were simply executed. Nobody knows how many Jews and other prisoners died on these death marches during the winter of 1944–1945. Estimates range from 250,000 to 375,000 victims.

By April 1945 the cruel winter had passed. Spring came and the German army surrendered. In a bunker deep under the streets of Berlin, Adolf Hitler killed himself. The war in Europe was over. However, the continent was in ruins. The major cities of Germany had been reduced to rubble. The population was scavenging for food and clothing. They were dependent on the occupying Allied forces for medicine and medical treatment.

There was little in the way of sympathy for the Germans in the immediate aftermath of the war. As Allied forces advancing from both east and west came upon the death camps, it seemed obvious that the Germans had committed a genocide of monstrous proportions. The first visual evidence left little doubt of that, and it was later confirmed by the records the Germans kept. Many Germans claimed they had no idea that mass murders had been taking place. The question then became: How could they not have known? The half million Jews who vanished from Germany itself, the manpower involved in carrying out the killings, the death trains—How could they not have known? Doubtless, some Germans genuinely didn't know. Nevertheless, for the majority of Germans alive during the war, the question remains unanswered.

The world at large was shocked by the revelations of the Holocaust. Nazi war criminals were rounded up and tried by the Allied powers at Nuremberg, Germany. The top Nazis were hanged, or committed suicide, or succeeded in fleeing. Most of the second-rank Nazis involved in the Holocaust escaped punishment, largely because the political climate changed. The threat to democracy now came from Russia. The Russians had established Communist puppet governments in Hungary, Czechoslovakia, and East Germany. It was thought necessary that the free nations establish West Germany as a democratic bulwark against communism. Dumping guilt on the German people by prosecuting ex-Nazis interfered with enlisting West German aid in the cold war against Communist Russia.

As a result of the Holocaust, the Jews of the world united in support of creating the Jewish homeland in Palestine, which we now know as Israel. The rest of the world turned its attention elsewhere—Korea, Vietnam, South Africa—to other trouble spots, other battles, other wars. Before long, for most people the Holocaust began to fade from memory.

AFTERWORD

This has been a book about those who committed the crimes of the Holocaust, not about the victims. However, in the fading memory of the Holocaust, some questions are raised again and again:

Why did the victims not fight back?

They did. There were uprisings in the camps and in the ghettoes. Jews were among the underground resistance groups who fought the Nazis in every country. Jewish groups were organized to rescue trapped families.

The devotion of Jewish families made it harder to fight back. The threat for the adult who fought was harm to his or her children, and death to aged parents. It was usually not clear that all would die until the very last moment, and by then loved ones were usually separated from one another. At different points in the rounding up and transporting and executing of the Jews, the techniques used by the Nazis to calm their victims' fears and trick them into believing they would survive were very effective. The Nazis were very good at devising lies that the Jews believed. After the war started, the Jews of the conquered countries were faced with an overwhelmingly superior armed force. Too often local populations collaborated with the Nazis in the destruction of the Jews. The Jews had neither the weapons nor the organization to fight the military killing squads effectively. The question is not why more didn't fight back, but how those who did fight back were able to do so in such terrible circumstances.

Why did they not flee?

Those who could, did. Often they found themselves in some other place where the Nazis had gained control. The first act the Nazis took against Jews was to seize their assets. There was no money for resettlement, no money for travel, and no money for bribes to get out of the country. It was often difficult to tell friend from foe.

In the beginning, in Germany, many Jews who might have fled did not do so because of their strong attachment to their country. Many had been German for generations. Both historically and in the twentieth century they had experienced outbreaks of anti-Semitism sweeping over Germany and had watched them recede. They knew that similar outbreaks occurred in other countries. They believed that the Nazi madness would pass and Germany would come to its senses.

For the Jews in other countries the question was not so much whether to flee, but where to go. In Western Europe many Jews fled to France only to be trapped there. Overseas countries wouldn't give them asylum and in any case, with the war on, there was no transport available. In Eastern Europe flight was frequently a prospect of "out of the Nazi frying pan and into the anti-Semitic fires" of such places as Hungary, the Ukraine, and Romania.

How anti-Semitic were the non-Nazis?

In Germany and in all the conquered nations there were non-Jewish individuals who defied the Nazis to help the Jews. Papers were forged and Jewish children enrolled in Catholic schools. Entire families of Jews were hidden in basements and attics. Food and medical care were provided. Catholic and Protestant clergy who protested the treatment of the Jews died in the death camps. Where some people all too gladly cooperated with the anti-Semitism of the Nazis, others risked their lives to oppose it. This was true of every nationality.

Were the Jews the only victims?

Not at all. The Nazis murdered Gypsy populations, Polish civilians, the citizens of entire villages in France and Czechoslovakia, Russian POWs, captured American fliers, homosexuals, mental patients, old people, and others. But the major population marked for killing were the Jews.

Six million Jews died. . . . Six million!

How can such a monstrous crime as the Holocaust occur? It begins when people start thinking of themselves as "us" and of others as "them." But there is no "us" and "them." There is only "we." Christians, Jews, Muslims, Buddhists, Hindus, Sikhs, atheists, agnostics, Africans, Asians, Europeans, Native Americans, Polynesians, and many, many more—all human beings.

There is only "*we*."

THE NAZIS AND THEIR FATE

After the war, the Allied powers convened courts and held trials at Nuremberg, Germany. Many top Nazis were charged with genocide and tried as war criminals. Those who had not been caught were tried *in absentia*. Their fates were varied.

Eichmann, Adolf—SS *Obersturmbannfuhrer* in charge of transporting Jews to the death camps. He was caught in Argentina by Israeli agents, tried, convicted, and hanged on May 31, 1962.

Frank, Hans—Nazi governor-general of the general government of Poland who urged that Jews be made "to disappear." He was tried for war crimes at Nuremberg and hanged on October 16, 1946.

Goebbels, Joseph—Anti-Semitic Nazi propaganda minister. At war's end, he and his wife committed suicide after first murdering their five children.

Göring, Reichsmarschall Hermann—Number two Nazi who created both the Gestapo and the concentration camps. On October 16, 1946, he committed suicide at Nuremberg while waiting to be hanged for war crimes.

Hess, Rudolf—Number three Nazi whom Hitler ordered shot on sight after he flew to England to try to make peace with the British in 1939. Hess received a life sentence as a war criminal and in 1987, at age ninety-three, committed suicide in prison.

Heydrich, Reinhard—Gestapo chief who organized the resettlement of Jews in ghettoes. He was killed by partisans near the Czech village of Lidice in June 1942.

Himmler, Heinrich—Head of the SS and Heydrich's boss, he was in charge of the concentration camps. Captured by the British at war's end, he killed himself by swallowing cyanide.

Hitler, Adolf—Der Führer—Head of the Nazi party; dictator of Germany and the lands it conquered. He committed suicide just before the war ended.

Hoess, Rudolf—Commandant of Auschwitz concentration camp. He was hanged at Auschwitz by the Poles in 1947.

Röhm, Ernst—Organizer and leader of the Nazi SA storm troopers, he was murdered by order of Hitler in June 1934.

Rosenberg, Alfred—Nazi "philosopher" and editor of the anti-Semitic *Voelkischer Beobachter*, he was convicted of war crimes and hanged at Nuremberg on October 16, 1946.

Strasser, Gregor—Hitler's rival for control of the Nazi party. He was murdered by Göring's order in June 1934.

Streicher, Julius—Whip-wielding editor of *Der Sturmer*, the most lurid of the anti-Jewish publications. He was hanged at Nuremberg on October 16, 1946. He died screaming anti-Semitic phrases and "Heil Hitler!"

CHRONOLOGY

1871—Prussian Chancellor Bismarck forms German states into a nation.

1889—April 20—Adolf Hitler is born.

1914—July 28—World War I begins.

1918—November 11—Germany is defeated; World War I ends.

1919—June 28—the Treaty of Versailles is signed.

1919—Hitler joins Germany Workers' Party, which will become Nazi party.

1919–1920—First *Reichstag* elected; Weimar Republic formed.

1923–1924—Beer Hall Putsch fails; Hitler writes *Mein Kampf* in prison.

1929—Depression strikes Germany.

1932—March 13—Hitler comes in second in presidential election with 30.1 percent of the vote.

1932—April 10—In a runoff election, Hitler gets 36.8 percent of the vote.

1933—January 30—President von Hindenburg names Hitler chancellor of Germany.

1933—February 27—Arson destroys the building where the *Reichstag* meets.

1933—First concentration camps built; Jews persecuted; books are burned; trade unions raided.

1934—June 30—"The Night of the Long Knives"—Hitler murders Nazi party rivals and dissidents.

1934—July—Nazis murder the chancellor of Austria.

1934—August—President von Hindenburg dies; Hitler combines offices of president and chancellor.

1934—August 19—90 percent of German voters approve Hitler as dictator.

1935—Coal-rich Saar district votes to rejoin Germany.

1935—September 15—Anti-Semitic Nuremberg Laws are passed.

1936—March 7—German army occupies the Rhineland.

1936—November 25—Germany, Italy, and Japan sign treaty forming Axis.

1938—March 14—German army invades Austria and is welcomed.

1938—April 10—99 percent of voters in both countries approve Germany annexing Austria.

1938—September 30—British prime minister Chamberlain agrees to German occupation of Czechoslovakia's Sudetenland in exchange for "peace in our time."

1938—October 5—German troops occupy Sudetenland.

1938—November 9–10—*Kristallnacht*: Jewish shops vandalized; synagogues destroyed.

1939—March 15—Hitler breaks promise to Chamberlain, seizes rest of Czechoslovakia.

1939—August 23—Nazi Germany and Communist Russia sign nonaggression pact.

1939—September 1—Nazi troops invade Poland; World War II begins.

1940—June—France and Norway surrender; British retreat from Dunkirk; Nazis control Europe.

1941—June 22—*Operation Barbarossa*—the German invasion of Russia—begins.

1941—July—Göring orders the "final solution of the Jewish question."

1941—December 7—Japanese warplanes bomb U.S. Navy ships at Pearl Harbor.

1941—December 11—The United States declares war on Japan's Axis partner, Germany.

1941–1942—July-March—One million Jews are murdered, mostly by firing squads made up of SS troops, German Order Police, and non-German "helpers."

1942—January—Wannsee Conference is held to arrange carrying out "final solution" more efficiently.

1942–April 1945—*Operation Reinhard*—the mass killing of millions of Jews in concentration camp gas chambers is carried out.

1945—April—Germany is defeated; Hitler commits suicide; the war in Europe ends.

SOURCE NOTES

Introduction

1. Alan Bullock, *Hitler and Stalin: Parallel Lives* (New York: Alfred A. Knopf, 1992), p. 974.
2. Joseph E. Persico, *Nuremberg: Infamy on Trial* (New York: Viking, 1994), p. 441.

Chapter One

1. Clara Leiser, ed., *Lunacy Becomes Us* (New York: Liveright Publishing Corporation, 1939), p. 73.
2. Alan Bullock, *Hitler and Stalin: Parallel Lives* (New York: Alfred A. Knopf, 1992), p. 147.
3. Ibid., p. 357.
4. Max I. Dimont, *Jews, God and History* (New York: Signet [paperback], 1962), p. 374.
5. Leiser, p. 111.
6. William L. Shirer, *The Rise and Fall of the Third Reich: A History of Nazi Germany* (New York: Simon & Schuster, 1960), p. 86.
7. Raul Hilberg, *Perpetrators Victims Bystanders: The Jewish Catastrophe 1933–1945* (New York: HarperCollins Publishers, 1992), p. 9.

8. Ibid.
9. Bullock, p. 357.
10. Ibid., p. 148.
11. Leiser, p. 122.

Chapter Two

1. *New Yorker*, Junc 3, 1996, p. 9.
2. Ibid., p. 8.
3. Ibid.
4. Donald S. Detwiler, *Germany: A Short History* (Carbondale, IL: Southern Illinois University Press [revised paperback edition], 1989), p. 170.
5. Ibid., p. 170.
6. Ibid., p. 171.
7. *Encyclopaedia Britannica,* Book 19 (Chicago: Encyclopaedia Britannica Inc., 1984), p. 967.
8. Ibid., p. 966.
9. Ibid.
10. Ibid.
11. Detwiler, p. 179.
12. *Encyclopaedia Britannica,* Book 8 (Chicago: Encyclopaedia Britannica Inc., 1984), p. 117.
13. William L. Shirer, *The Rise and Fall of the Third Reich: A History of Nazi Germany* (New York: Simon & Schuster, 1960), p. 68.
14. Ibid., p. 70.
15. Ibid., p. 74

Chapter Three

1. Alan Bullock, *Hitler and Stalin: Parallel Lives* (New York: Alfred A. Knopf, 1992), p. 137.

2. Adolf Hitler, *Mein Kampf* (Boston: Houghton Mifflin [English translation uncredited], 1943), p. 6.
3. Ibid., p. 10.
4. Ibid.
5. Bullock, p. 8.
6. Ibid., p. 23.
7. Ibid., p. 19.
8. Raul Hilberg, *Perpetrators Victims Bystanders: The Jewish Catastrophe 1933–1945* (New York: HarperCollins Publishers, 1992), p. 5.
9. Bullock, p. 71.
10. *Encyclopaedia Britannica,* Book 8 (Chicago: Encyclopaedia Britannica Inc., 1984), p. 966.
11. Ibid.
12. Ibid.
13. Daniel Jonah Goldhagen, *Hitler's Willing Executioners: Ordinary Germans and the Holocaust* (New York: Alfred A. Knopf, 1996), p. 85.
14. Hitler, p. 679.
15. *Encyclopaedia Britannica,* p. 967.
16. Bullock, p. 368.

Chapter Four

1. William L. Shirer, *The Rise and Fall of the Third Reich: A History of Nazi Germany* (New York: Simon & Schuster, 1960), p. 36.
2. Ibid.
3. Ibid.
4. Ibid.
5. *Encyclopaedia Britannica,* Book 8 (Chicago: Encyclopaedia Britannica Inc., 1984), p. 637.
6. Ibid.
7. Shirer, p. 38.

8. Ibid., p. 39.

9. Ibid.

10. Ibid.

11. Daniel Jonah Goldhagen, *Hitler's Willing Executioners: Ordinary Germans and the Holocaust* (New York: Alfred A. Knopf, 1996), p. 82.

12. Ibid.

13. Ibid.

14. Ibid., p. 83.

15. Ibid.

16. Ibid.

17. Shirer, p. 49.

18. Ibid., p. 48.

19. Alan Bullock, *Hitler and Stalin: Parallel Lives* (New York: Alfred A. Knopf, 1992), p. 82.

20. Ibid., p. 83.

21. Shirer, p. 48.

22. Bullock, p. 81.

23. Shirer, p. 123.

24. Ibid., p. 127.

25. Ibid., p. 126.

26. Ibid., p. 127.

27. Ibid., p.128.

Chapter Five

1. William L. Shirer, *The Rise and Fall of the Third Reich: A History of Nazi Germany* (New York: Simon & Schuster, 1960), p. 155.

2. Ibid., p. 173.

3. *Chronicles of the 20th Century* (Mount Kisco, NY: Chronicle Publications, 1987), p. 415.

4. Ibid., p. 416.

5. *Encyclopaedia Britannica*, Book 8 (Chicago: Encyclopaedia Britannica Inc., 1984), p. 486.

6. Ibid.

7. Joseph E. Persico, *Nuremberg: Infamy on Trial* (New York: Viking, 1994), p. 106.

8. *Chronicles of the 20th Century*, p. 419.

9. Ibid., p. 420.

10. Ibid., p. 421.

11. Raul Hilberg, *Perpetrators Victims Bystanders: The Jewish Catastrophe 1933–1945* (New York: HarperCollins Publishers, 1992), p. 67.

12. *Chronicles of the 20th Century*, p. 425.

13. Shirer, p. 263.

14. Ibid., p. 216.

15. *Chronicles of the 20th Century*, p. 433.

16. Shirer, p. 223.

17. Ibid., p. 225.

18. Ibid.

19. Ibid., p. 227.

20. *Chronicles of the 20th Century*, p. 442.

21. Ibid.

22. Ibid., p. 446.

23. Ibid.

24. *The New York Times*, June 18, 1996, p. B12.

25. Ibid.

26. *Chronicles of the 20th Century*, p. 454.

Chapter Six

1. Hitler, Adolf, *Mein Kampf* (Boston: Houghton Mifflin [English translation uncredited], 1943), p. 138–139.

2. Ibid.

3. *Chronicles of the 20th Century* (Mount Kisco, NY: Chronicle Publications, 1987), p. 464.

4. Gunter Grau, tr. Patrick Camiller, *Hidden Holocaust?* (New York: Cassell, 1995), p. 135.

5. Donald S. Detwiler, *Germany: A Short History* (Carbondale, IL: Southern Illinois University Press [revised paperback edition], 1989), p. 195.

6. *Chronicles of the 20th Century*, p. 483.

7. Ibid., p. 485.

8. *Encyclopaedia Britannica*, Book 2 (Chicago: Encyclopaedia Britannica Inc., 1984), p. 717.

9. Ibid.

10. *Chronicles of the 20th Century*, p. 486.

11. William L. Shirer, *The Rise and Fall of the Third Reich: A History of Nazi Germany* (New York: Simon & Schuster, 1960), p. 430.

12. Joseph E. Persico, *Nuremberg: Infamy on Trial* (New York: Viking, 1994), p. 283.

13. Ibid.

14. Ibid., p. 203.

15. Ibid., p. 202.

16. *Chronicles of the 20th Century*, p. 493.

17. Ibid.

Chapter Seven

1. Daniel Jonah Goldhagen, *Hitler's Willing Executioners: Ordinary Germans and the Holocaust* (New York: Alfred A. Knopf, 1996), p. 145.

2. Raul Hilberg, *Perpetrators Victims Bystanders: The Jewish Catastrophe 1933–1945* (New York: HarperCollins Publishers, 1992), p. 203.

3. Ibid.

4. Hannah Arendt, *Eichmann in Jerusalem: A Report on the Banality of Evil* (New York: Penguin Books [paperback], 1994), p. 171.

5. Ibid., p. 185.
6. Ibid., p. 187.
7. Ibid., p. 179.
8. William L. Shirer, *The Rise and Fall of the Third Reich: A History of Nazi Germany* (New York: Simon & Schuster, 1960), p. 964.

Chapter Eight

1. Christopher R. Browning, *Ordinary Men: Reserve Police Battalion 101 and the Final Solution in Poland* (New York: HarperCollins Publishers, 1992), p. xv.
2. Daniel Jonah Goldhagen, *Hitler's Willing Executioners: Ordinary Germans and the Holocaust* (New York: Alfred A. Knopf, 1996) p. 149.
3. Raul Hilberg, *Perpetrators Victims Bystanders: The Jewish Catastrophe 1933–1945* (New York: HarperCollins Publishers, 1992), p. 58.
4. Goldhagen, p. 188.
5. Yitzhak Arad, *Belzec, Sobibor, Treblinka: The Operation Reinhard Death Camps* (Bloomington, IN: Indiana University Press, 1987), p.10.

Chapter Nine

1. Yitzhak Arad, *Belzec, Sobibor, Treblinka: The Operation Reinhard Death Camps* (Bloomington, IN: Indiana University Press, 1987), p. 12.
2. Ibid., p. 13.
3. *Chronicles of the 20th Century* (Mount Kisco, NY: Chronicle Publications, 1987), p. 538.
4. Arad, p. 14.
5. William L. Shirer, *The Rise and Fall of the Third Reich: A History of Nazi Germany* (New York: Simon & Schuster, 1960), p. 968.
6. Ibid.
7. Ibid.
8. Ibid., p. 971.

9. Ibid.

10. Hannah Arendt, *Eichmann in Jerusalem: A Report on the Banality of Evil* (New York: Penguin Books [paperback], 1994), p. 79.

11. Shirer, p. 969.

12. Christopher R. Browning, *Ordinary Men: Reserve Police Battalion 101 and the Final Solution in Poland* (New York: HarperCollins Publishers, 1992), p. 50.

13. Joseph E. Persico, *Nuremberg: Infamy on Trial* (New York: Viking, 1994), p. 318.

GLOSSARY

Anschluss — unification of Germany and Austria

Beer Hall Putsch — the failed Nazi attempt to organize an overthrow of the Weimar Republic

blitzkrieg — a sudden and overwhelming attack; a drive that can't be stopped

chancellor — the prime minister in charge of running the German government

concentration camp — a place of confinement for anti-Nazis and Jews; workplace; slaughterhouse

death camps — those concentration camps equipped for mass killing

death marches — the Nazi practice of herding prisoners from camps at war's end; many died

Einsatzgruppen — SS squads assigned to murdering Jews and others

final solution — the Nazi plan to kill off the entire Jewish population of Europe

führer — national leader; Adolf Hitler was *Der Führer* (the leader) of Germany

gas vans — trucks with sealed compartments used to murder victims by carbon monoxide poisoning

general government of Poland — the western regions of Poland conquered by the Germans

genocide — the killing of a whole race, people, or nation

Gestapo — the Nazi secret police active in rounding up Jews for the death camps

ghetto — originally an area where Jews were forced to live

guerrilla — volunteer member of a small group fighting the occupying Nazi army

Holocaust — systematic extermination of six million European Jews by the Nazis

Judenrein — free of Jews

Lebensraum — "room to live"; Hitler's policy of seizing land for German use

Mein Kampf (*My Struggle*) — Hitler's blend of autobiography and anti-Semitic call to arms

Operation *Erntefest* (Harvest Ball) — the Nazi killing of large numbers of slave laborers

Operation Barbarossa — the German invasion of Russia in June 1941

Operation Reinhard — the Nazi plan for the organized killing of Eastern European Jews

Order Police — reserve police units who helped round up and kill Eastern European Jews

Reichstag — the German parliament

SA (*Sturmabteilung*) — Ernst Röhm's private army of Nazi storm troopers active in the 1920s

Schutzmannschaft — volunteers in Nazi-occupied countries who helped the SS slaughter Jews

slave labor — Jewish, Polish, Czech, and other prisoners forced to work in German industry

Sonderkommandos — Jewish death-camp prisoners assigned to disposing of corpses of victims

SS (*Schutzstaffel*) — Hitler's personal guard unit; expanded in the war to perform mass killings

synagogue — Jewish house of worship

Wannsee Conference — 1942 meeting of Nazi leaders to plan how to kill Jews more efficiently

Weimar Republic — Germany between the fall of the kaiser and the rise to power of Hitler

Zyklon-B — the crystals used to make the gas used for mass killings

FOR MORE INFORMATION

Browning, Christopher R., *Ordinary Men: Reserve Police Battalion 101 and the Final Solution in Poland*. New York: HarperCollins Publishers, 1992.

Bullock, Alan, *Hitler and Stalin: Parallel Lives*. New York: Alfred A. Knopf, 1992.

Bytwerk, Randall L., *Julius Streicher: The Man Who Persuaded a Nation to Hate Jews*. New York: Dorset Press, 1983.

Frank, Anne, *Anne Frank: The Diary of a Young Girl*. New York: Pocket Books [paperback], 1953.

Handler, Andrew, and Susan V. Meschel, *Young People Speak: Surviving the Holocaust*. Danbury, CT: Franklin Watts, 1993.

Keneally, Thomas, *Schindler's List*. New York: Simon & Schuster, 1982.

Kuznetsov, Anatoly, *Babi Yar*. New York: Dell, 1967.

Landau, Elaine, *We Survived the Holocaust*. Danbury, CT: Franklin Watts, 1991.

Lobel, Anita, *No Pretty Pictures: A Child of War*. New York: Greenwillow, 1998.

Opdyke, Irene Gut, and Jennifer Armstrong, *In My Hands: Memories of a Holocaust Rescuer*. New York: Random, 1998.

Persico, Joseph E., *Nuremberg: Infamy on Trial.* New York: Viking, 1994.

Rochman, Hazel, and Darlene Z. Campbell, eds. *Bearing Witness: Stories of the Holocaust*. New York: Orchard, 1995.

Shirer, William L., *The Rise and Fall of the Third Reich: A History of Nazi Germany.* New York: Simon & Schuster, 1960.

Spencer, William, *Germany Then and Now.* Danbury, CT: Franklin Watts, 1994.

Yoran, Shalom, *The Defiant: A Triumphant Tale of Jewish Vengeance and Survival.* New York: St. Martin's Press, 1996.

Internet Sites

(All have links to related sites.)

The Jewish Student Online Research Center (JSOURCE)
www.us-israel.org/jsource

Holocaust Resources on the World Wide Web
www.fred.net/nhhs/html/hololink.htm

The United States Holocaust Memorial Museum
www.ushmm.org

Remembering the Holocaust
  yarra.vicnet.net.au/~aragorn/holocaus.htm

The Holocaust: A Historical Summary
  www.ushmm.org/education/history.html

INDEX